My Recovery Way

As We Trudge the Road:

From Alcohol Abuse to the Heroin and Prescription Opioid Epidemic and Surviving a Traumatic Brain Injury

Darren H.

Copyright © 2020 Darren H.
All rights reserved
First Edition

NEWMAN SPRINGS PUBLISHING
320 Broad Street
Red Bank, NJ 07701

First originally published by Newman Springs Publishing 2020

ISBN 978-1-64801-474-1 (Paperback)
ISBN 978-1-64801-475-8 (Digital)

Printed in the United States of America

For The Millions Of People Trying To
Live Life One Day At A Time.

On the nineteenth of March, 2014, at 4:00 a.m., I was woken by a loud crash upstairs. My girlfriend, Sara, who was lying next to me on my bed downstairs, said, "Put your sweats on, something's happening."

The next thing I heard was my locked doorknob trying to be turned, then that awful gut-wrenching sound of my door being kicked open and the sight of six cops with clear shields on their faces and rifles in their hands surrounding the bed! Sara was sitting up on the side of the bed, and I was lying on my back.

The officer in charge said, "Roll over and put your hands behind you!"

I did what I was told and I was handcuffed as another cop cuffed Sara. As our rights were read to us, I was then pulled off the bed. I said, "Please put my shoes on me, I have a head injury that makes me very off balance, and I need them to walk."

After he let me step into my shoes, we were taken up the stairs and led into the front room where all nine of my roommates were also cuffed and sitting on the couches. The officer in charge pulled a warrant out of his pocket; he looked down at it and said, "I have a warrant for Darren H. in possession of heroin."

Suddenly I became the most important person in the house. My ego loved it. The hateful stares from my cuffed roommates I will never forget. They sat Sara down on one of the couches and then took me into the kitchen. I was sat down on a stool by the wall as I looked over at the kitchen table. I saw three more cops sitting there. Two of them were on laptops, and the third was on a phone. The officer in charge said to me, "We're going to search your entire house, but it will be a lot nicer for you if you tell me where and what we're going to find."

Memories of the couple years I spent in the penitentiary in the mid-nineties came rushing over me, so I felt like I should be as cooperative as I could be, so I told him, "There's sixty twenties of black in my front right pocket of my jeans on the floor in my room, and there's a quarter ounce of go-fast in the lockbox on the floor in the closet, and in that same box is fifteen-gram bags of medical marijuana."

After about an hour sitting on that stool in the kitchen, the officer running the show came back upstairs and thanked me for telling him the location of all the dope. He then said, "You have enough of three different controlled substances that we're going to charge you with three distribution charges." He then told me, "Because this house sits 525 feet east of the Kearns Elementary School, we're going to enhance the charges from second-degree to first-degree felonies, and we also found $700 cash in your jeans pocket."

I politely asked if I could have some of my cash to put on my books.

He said, "No." I was then walked out of the kitchen through the roommate-filled living room and out the front door and into the back of one of the many cop cars that were parked in the driveway.

I had been in a daze since I woke to the loud noise upstairs and wasn't really sure if I was awake or in a dream, but when they booked me into the jail and I was given my booking sheet that read the same sentence on three different lines—"Distribution of Controlled Substance, First-Degree Felony 5 to Life"—I realized then that I was wide awake! After reading those words, I got very sad and I began to get tears in my eyes. Memories of the years I spent down twenty years ago consumed me.

As I waited for them to call me up for my mug shot, I was able to call my mother on the phone. I think I cried as much as she did for about ten minutes. I was then called over for my picture to be taken, and then they issued me a wheelchair. I waited for about three hours for them to dress me and take me to quarantine where I stayed for five days, and then to D-pod, my new home. After a couple days in my new home, I thought I'd start writing about my life.

I was born on the second of July, 1969, in Salt Lake City, Utah. My folks were divorced when I was about a year old. I guess my first memory of life was when I was four or five. My mom was remarried to my two little sisters' dad. His name was Dan. My memory is not telling me how I felt, just the action that took place. I still see my mother, Phoebe, standing in the doorway of Dan's office, crying at me or with me as I lay across Dan's lap with my pants down, and he whipping my butt with his belt. Life with Dan and that belt of his lasted just a few years...well, that I remember anyway.

The year 1977 was the one when I first felt grown up. I remember going to my first movie without my mom, *Star Wars, Episode Four*. A couple months after, in July, I turned eight, so I was baptized in to the Mormon Church, a real growing experience. I then bought my first album, "Love Gun" by KISS. I joined the KISS Army shortly thereafter. Then the following month, I felt my first rejection by a woman. I was over at my friends' house, David and Michel. We were playing hide and seek, and I was hiding under the back of an old truck that was in there backyard. One of the brothers released the tailgate, and as the door swung down, I was standing up. As the blood and tears ran down both my cheeks, the three of us ran into their house.

David yelled, "Mom, Darren's bleeding!"

Their mom was sitting in front of the black and white television. We got no response. So again, he said, "Mom, Darren's bleeding."

She didn't even turn around. I remember how sad her voice sounded when she said, "Elvis Presley just died!"

The move away from Salt Lake was really just a move away from that violent stepfather of mine. The first altering of my mind felt proper because of the freedom I now felt being away from what or whom I feared so much. My mom, my three sisters, and I moved to an apartment complex in North Kansas City, Missouri. Phoebe, my mom, had an old guy friend that lived there in Kansas City. His name was Clyde. That's why we moved so far away from what she knew. In the complex, there were a few recreational spots for the kids to play. There were Jungle Gyms, slippery slides, swings, and something I didn't know much about, boys to play and hang with. I could leave my sister's home with Mom and venture out in the hood with the fellows. I must have been a pretty cool eight-year-old.

I hung out with the ten and twelve-year-olds. They—or we—grew pot back behind the apartments in the field by the woods. Most of my new friends were African American. I remember a couple Spanish kids, but I don't recall there being any white kids, but there must have been some. Oh, wait, except for Mary. She was the first girl I ever kissed. She was white and stunning. The kids that I hung out with would steal alcohol from their parents. My mom didn't drink. Not real sure how they would always get it so easily, but they did.

We would soak down the freshly picked pot leaves with the alcohol and then lay the wet pot on a big thin piece of wood in the sun. We would come back the next day and retrieve the pot, which was always dried out completely. We would then crumble down the dried pot in our hands, roll it up in a rolling paper, and smoke it.

I went to court today and talked to my attorney about my options, then I instructed her to tell the judge that I was willing to do drug court. After she informed the judge that I will be applying for drug court, my next court date was set up. She, Judge Ruby Mills, set my next court date out to about thirty days. Then she reduced my bail from $50,000 to $25,000, which was still way to high of an amount to even think about a bonding out. Now drug court seemed like the best option because once completed, my charges would be dropped off my record or reduced to misdemeanors anyway.

She, my attorney, thinks she can keep me from going back to prison. She says that the President Barack Obama is on a mission. He's trying to push programs over prisons. I told her that I was in a rally or a march back in the late 80s up State Street to the capital here in Salt Lake City. About forty or fifty of us from CA (12-Step Fellowship) with picket signs in our hands chanted "More Treatment, Less Prisons, More Treatment, and Less Prisons." We got all three local news channels up to the capitol. But nothing ever changed; just more money went in to prisons. Before she left, she said to me, "Hopefully, the president can make it happen for you."

MY RECOVERY WAY

Before I went to sleep that night, I put my hands together and bowed my head and prayed for Gods will to be done, something I used to do every night but hadn't in a couple years.

*****

It's almost 7:00 a.m. here on Delta block, and its Sunday morning. We just finished breakfast and have now racked back in our cells. My roommates name is Tomcat, and he's here on a probation violation. He has a release date in June sometime. Sundays here in the County Jail seem just like every other day here in paradise except for the AA meeting. This meeting has made Sunday my favorite day.

Terry comes in from the outside and runs the meeting. Terry and I have been friends for twenty-five years. I met Terry in the rooms of AA (12-Step Fellowship) in 1988; we had both just gotten sober.

*****

I was first arrested in 1981 when I was twelve years old. The charge was possession of alcohol by a minor. We had moved back to Utah from Kansas City. We were living in Bountiful, Utah, about seven miles north of Salt Lake. I was at the Rustic Roller-Skating Rink with my friend, Brian. Brian was fifteen. It seemed that all my friends growing up were always a few years older than I. We were standing out front of the rink in a big circle of people. I was handed a mason jar by the guy standing next to me. He said, "Drink this."

So of course, I did. Well, I tried to anyway. I poured it into my mouth, but it would not go down my throat. It was too strong. So it came back out and onto the ground. The crowd chuckled. That was my first taste of Everclear. Brian and I were walking home from the roller-skating rink. We walked through a parking lot in a strip mall called Colonial Square. While walking, a cop pulled up and asked us what we were doing. I don't know what I said, but I did speak. My breath must have smelled like alcohol, so I was handcuffed and put into the back of the police car. The cop then drove me to the Bountiful police station.

My mother was then called and told to come down and pick me up. I don't remember even speaking with my mother about drinking alcohol. When she came and picked me up from the Bountiful police station, I'm sure she asked, and I'm sure I just told her it was an accident that alcohol made it into my mouth that night. When I went to the Third District Juvenile Court, I was given a fine for $35. The charge was possession of alcohol by a minor. The judge also put me on probation.

The week after my first arrest, I lost my virginity. Her name was Gwen, and she was seventeen years old. We were both over at Brian's and we were walking home together. Somehow, we ended up in the bushes outside a big white church. I didn't know what I was doing, but she sure did. It was fun, an experience I'll never forget. Don't think I was quite old enough to have an orgasm because I didn't, but it sure felt good.

I was first introduced to pill form narcotics in 1981. I was twelve years old and I was hanging out with some friends one night in the trailer court where they lived. The trailer court sat on the west side of Highway 89 in North Salt Lake. On the east side was the grocery store where we would steal cigarettes. We were headed over across the highway. My friends, Paul and Francis, took off running, and my shoe came off, so I took just a few seconds to put it back on. I then took off behind my buddies but then stopped just shortly past the middle of the road and waited for the motorcycle to fly by so I could cross.

When the motorcycle got about fifty feet from me, I could tell it wasn't a motorcycle but a little Volkswagen bug with its driver's side headlight burned out. It was a good disguise because it fooled me. I quickly tried to jump out of the way but not quick enough. The little disguised Volkswagen bug was doing fifty miles an hour and caught my right hip. I flew about thirty feet down the road. I remember the lady, who was a passenger in the car, crying so much and all the cops and my first ambulance ride to the Lakeview Hospital in Bountiful. The doctor told me that I'd chipped a disk in the bottom of my back and that the nerves in my back may get pinched in that chip.

So I was given Carisoprodol (Soma) muscle relaxers and I was prescribed them whenever I needed them. Certain activities I would do would cause those nerves in my back to be pinched, and I would have to arch my back to pull the lower back forward to be able to withstand the pain. I would eat a Soma that would always put me right to sleep, and when I awoke, the pain was gone, truly a miracle drug.

On the ninth of January 1982, I went to my first rock concert. It was Ozzy Osbourne, the "Diary of a Madman" tour, with Randy Rhodes on lead guitar. My buddy, Brian, took me to the show and bought me a ticket. We had upper bowl seats, but when the lights were turned down, we jumped the railing and made our way slowly through the crowd up to about the third row. I remember standing on a chair next to Brian, and we were smoking a joint. We were so close to the stage I could almost touch Randy Rhodes.

The stage was set up to where it looked like the outside of a big castle. Up in one of the castle windows was a man in a hooded monk's robe playing an organ. In the middle of the stage was a white staircase, and at the top of the staircase was where the drums sat. At the end of the concert, for the encore, the stairs lifted up, and a big white hand with Ozzy sitting in the middle of it came out. I was so high but will never forget my first concert. Randy Rhodes died a couple months after that on the nineteenth of March 1982. That was an absolute loss for the entire world.

A few weeks before Randy Rhodes died, I went skiing with my dad. We went to Solitude Ski Resort up Big Cottonwood Canyon. My father and I had a friendly relationship. I would see him a few times a month or so. My father was on his third marriage to a wonderful lady named Patrica. They were married in July of 1981. Patrica had two little boys, Samuel and Thomas. They were very religious and members of the LDS church.

After we were done skiing for the day, we went to my dad's house and waited for my mom to arrive to pick me up. When she arrived, it was strange because she got out of her car and walked to the door. She had never done that before. She didn't ever want to be in the same room as my father. As she approached the door, Gary, my dad, said, "Darren, we need to talk to you." Patrica, my stepmom, my mom, my dad, and I all went in to the guest bedroom. My dad spoke first. He said, "Darren, we have decided it would be best for everyone if you came and lived here with us."

Then my mom spoke. She said, "Darren, I received a call from South Davis Junior High School, and the lady said you have thirty-eight truancies this quarter."

My father then said, "While you live here, you will attend all your classes every day and you will do homework every night and you will get no lower than a C or you will be grounded." My big sister, Kimberly, was forced to come live out at my dad's house shortly after I. She was a hell-raiser as well.

My first arrest, after I moved in with my dad, was just at a party that got busted for being loud and ended with another charge for underaged drinking. These kinds of parties happened all the time with the new friends I made; well, eventually made. I would make friends with kids my own age first and then would always end up befriending their older siblings. I just always meshed better with a slightly older crowd.

I had a friend named Derrick who would travel back and forth to Las Vegas a few times a month. Derrick introduced me to a special drug called Quaaludes. What made them so special was because if I ate one and drank a couple beers, it made me feel like I just drank a twelve-pack. My first and best friend at that time was Mark. We hit it off so well because we both loved to smoke pot. His big brother, Frank, and his friends always had it. When we had none of our own and Frank wasn't around, we would scrape his bong.

Mark and I hung out together at school for about eighteen months. The reason I say hung out at school was because I got grounded after the first report card came out, and I remained grounded for my entire stay at my dad's. This gave me a love for school because it got me out of the house. Mark was a year younger than I, so I left middle school a year before him. Sometime before our split, I had bought a quarter ounce of pot from Kevin, one of Mark's brother Frank's bros. I got the $25 to pay for it from my dad's wallet while he was in the shower. My plan was to split the quarter up into seven grams, then sell six of them for $10 each and keeping a gram for myself. I then planned on spending $45 of the $60 on a half-ounce and then just keep increasing the amount of profit I would make by the more pot I would have for sale. It sounded like a perfect plan to me.

The buses arrived anywhere from 7:35 to 7:45, and school started at 8:00 a.m. I had walked to school that day, which I usually did, for it gave me more time to smoke. I was standing out in front of the school when the first bus arrived. My buddy, Wesley, got off that first bus and bought three grams from me at $10 each, which he immediately turned around and sold for $15 each. I could already tell this was my new profession. I also sold the three remaining grams to three different people at $10 each before the eight o'clock bell rang. On my way to class, I told my buddy, Mark, to meet me in the bathroom during the first ten minutes of second period.

Second period was my math class. I was always very good at math, so I didn't mind missing a bit of it once in a while. I told the teacher, Mrs. Whatever Her Name Was, that my stomach was killing me and I really needed to go to the bathroom. She agreed and let me go. I met Mark in the bathroom, and he had already constructed a pipe out of a toilet paper roll and a piece of tinfoil. I loaded a bowl out of my remaining gram of pot, and we proceeded to smoke it. When we finished, we were both baked and we headed back to our classes. After math ended and I was walking to third period, English, the hallway wreaked like pot so bad, I was so proud.

I loved English with Mrs. Anderson. She was so beautiful, her eyes always sparkled, and she had enormous breasts! About halfway through my favorite class, Mr. Beverage, the vice principal, got on the intercom and said, "Will all the teachers who had a second period class please send up a list of all the students who left class during the period. Thank you." I knew I was fucked.

Ten minutes later, someone from the office came in and said I was wanted at Mr. Cochever's office. He was the principal, which was good because he was nicer than Mr. Beverage. When I arrived, it didn't matter who was nicer because they were both in the office along with a man wearing a gun. Mr. Beverage then said, "Sit down, Darren, this is Officer Maxwell. He's here to talk to you." I thought they were going to talk to me about smoking pot in the bathroom during second period. That wasn't even important to them at that time. There was a rat disguised as a boy named Chris who bought a gram from Wesley, and his only reason for buying this gram was so that he could roll over on Wesley and get him busted. Wesley was my friend and he never wanted to get me in trouble, but we were just thirteen years old. I don't blame him for getting scared and telling Maxwell where he got the weed. Rolling over on someone like that is something I could never do, but I don't blame Wesley. He was just a scared kid.

*****

Convicts are very clean people in captivity. Every day after lunch here in D block, the trustees pass out about ten feet of paper towels to the thirty-two cells. Then they pass around the blue spray bottle of Windex and the green bottle of some kind of cleaning agent. The broom then circulates, followed by the mop and bucket. The desks, windows, and floors never really get dirty, but we clean them with all our might whenever we can. It's Monday night here in Delta pod, and I don't think there is any Bible study tonight, so maybe I can win some soups playing spades. I only have one phone call left on my card until I get my commissary on Friday, so I'll try and call Sara tonight. God, I hope we're not locked down.

*****

I remember thinking how strange it was and how long I had wait for each authority to come speak to me. By the time Maxwell had read me my rights and I had the cute silver bracelets around my wrists, the 2:30 end of seventh period bell had rung. The halls were filled with hundreds of innocent little children. I see now that was the point of taking so long to arrest me. Officer Maxwell walked me with my hands cuffed behind my back through the crowded hallway and out the front door to the police car. He then sat me down in the backseat and shut the back door. He walked around and got in the driver's side. He grabbed his radio, pushed the button, and said, "Beta 4 Maxwell here, have one juvenile in custody en route for detention."

The drive was fast from Sandy to South Salt Lake. I was surprised to see, after we arrived at the detention center, another car arrive carrying Chris and Wesley. I was sure I made the trip alone. There were seven holding cells at the front of the detention center. We took up three, and the other four were empty. We sat alone in our separate cells for about an hour. We were unable to speak to each other. It must have been Chris's mom that showed up first for him, and then Wesley's parents came for him. I started to get a little excited for I knew I was next. I was a little confused when the man approached my cell door because I hadn't seen anyone arrive for me yet. The man said, "Darren, let's get you get showered in."

I said, "What do you mean? Why do Wesley and Chris get to go home and I don't?"

He then told me because I was charged with distribution, and the only way I could leave was if a judge said so, and since it was 4:45 on Friday afternoon, I couldn't see the judge until Monday morning.

*****

It's 5:15 a.m. on Tuesday morning. They just turned on the lights on here in D-pod. Breakfast is not for an hour, but they liked to give us plenty of time to think, I guess, about the error of our ways, why we were here, or what we should have done differently. I wonder if this is beneficial or not. I always believed that when an addict was alone, they were in bad company. Generally, my thoughts are on recovery. I do believe it to be the easier, softer way to do life here in lock up. When people find out why I'm here and ask to read my court papers with my charges listed, they kind of praise me and ask to work with me. It's real hard to push the tone of recovery onto people who want to make money for themselves by selling dope, which in return makes money for me. But deep inside my gut, I know I will never be successful at slinging dope. I will eventually start using again. I'm sure it will kill me!

*****

DARREN H.

The man at the detention center opened my cell and said, "Darren, let's get you showered and get you back to N section." After I showered, I put on the detention center clothes, which included tighty-whities that I never wore. I was a boxer boy.

I was walked down a long hallway. We stopped at a door labeled N. The man removed a large set of keys from his waist and opened the door to a large room. There was nobody in the room, but there was a couch, a chair, a bookshelf, and a TV. The man told me this was the dayroom. He then told me that we were on lockdown for dinner. He said, "You will get you a tray once we get you back to the room."

I then followed him down another hallway where we stopped at another door labeled 23. He unlocked the door, and we walked in. There was a bed, a sink, a toilet, and a window with a screen so thick you couldn't see out. The man then told me, "Your first twenty-four hours will be spent in solitary confinement." Solitary confinement became illegal for kids in 1985. It was now 1983, so they could still do it.

For twenty-four hours, I cried like a little girl. I cried and counted the bricks in three of the four walls. There was nothing else to do. They made sure of that. Someone would come and slide my meals under the door. The only way to keep track of time was counting the trays. After I received my fourth tray, I knew the solitary would be over soon. I was so happy to hear the rattle sound of keys and the unlocking of the big green door that kept me caged in. The walls down the hall back to the dayroom seemed so nice and different than the walls in my room. The dayroom had fifteen boys, mostly Spanish or Mexican, a few African Americans, and a couple of white kids. They were watching TV and goofing off. There were four adults sitting around the kids.

I stayed in detention from Friday until Monday when the courts opened again and I could see a judge. I was put on a two-week house arrest. Living with my father was kind of like being in detention; food was a lot better though. It was the middle of December; school was on Christmas break. I had no reason to leave the house, which meant no smoking. Once in a great while, Patrica, my stepmom, would go to the store or to an appointment. I would smoke as much as possible while she was gone. I would stand on the side of the house and gaze toward the bottom of our circle, waiting to see that big green van that she drove. Once I would see the van, I would run to the back of the house and in through the sliding glass door, then into the bathroom, and start brushing my teeth and washing the smoke smell off my face and hands.

I had a friend named Derek. He was a couple years younger than I, but I liked to hang with him because his mom would buy us cigarettes and let us smoke in the house. Derek and I liked to get high together and drink alcohol. He was a brittle diabetic; he had no pancreas. Derek really had to watch his sugar intake, which made drinking my favorite wine, Mad Dog 20/20, almost impossible. He was always in the hospital because of the sugar level in his blood.

Derek and I used to race our BMX bikes together in the mid-eighties. I played a lot of soccer at this time in my life. I was super-fast on my feet. It was also an acceptable reason to leave the house, which meant I could smoke cigarettes and pot on my walk to and from soccer practice. Most Saturdays, after my games, I would get home, and my nerves in my back were usually being pinched in my chipped disk—something about using the muscles to run would affect the nerves in my back—so I would eat a Soma and sleep until the next morning.

When I was fourteen years old, my probation officer mentioned to me that it might be beneficial for me to attend an AA meeting. Oddly enough, my older friend, Trevor, had just gotten his first DUI and was having his mom take him to a noon meeting at a place called Fellowship Hall, and he asked me if I'd go with him. I, of course, said yes, not because I wanted to go to my first AA meeting, but because it was a legitimate reason to leave the house so I could smoke. My dad was okay with me going because my probation officer had suggested it.

Fellowship Hall was an old rundown building that looked like a big house. It sat on about 15th South, just west of Main Street, on a road called Richard Street in downtown Salt Lake. Every other guy in the meeting was at least fifty years older than I, and there were no ladies; how could this possibly benefit me? There were four long tables in the room in the shape of a square with nothing in the middle, so we all just kind of faced each other. When the meeting started, certain parts were read out of a book, and then we were asked to introduce ourselves. All the others said their names and that they were alcoholic, but not me. I thought that was stupid. I just said, "My name is Darren and I'm here with Trevor."

A few different guys shared about things in their lives, but then a man named Blaine with long white hair and a long white beard shared. Blaine talked about a disease he had called alcoholism. He talked about a *mental obsession* that he would have for a drink, and then the *phenomenon of craving* would take over, and he had no ability to stop. I knew exactly what this old drunk was talking about. That was exactly what happened to me every time. I always tell myself that it will be different this time or I would tell myself that I would only have a couple but would always drink until I blacked out. Could I be an alcoholic like Blaine, the old white-haired man?

I think I actually drank more after my first AA meeting than I did before it. I now had an understanding of the disease that the white-haired Blaine and I had. It kind of made it okay to drink like I did. It wasn't my fault it was a disease. It's normal for people like me to drink like I did.

Shortly after my first AA meeting, I stole a check out of my dad's dresser drawer and gave it to a friend of my sister's named Chris, and she forged it for a case of beer. Chris and I would sleep together every time she would stay over with my sister. She was a lot of fun. When my dad got the forged check back from the bank, he told me that he couldn't afford to keep me living there any longer and I was free to go. I moved right in with Derek and his mom, Josie, and his sister, Stephanie. I felt a true freedom being away from all the rules I was forced to follow at my dad's.

I fell in love for the first time shortly after that. Derek and I were at the fireworks show at the Sugarhouse Park. It was the celebration on July 4, 1984. I had just come out of the bathroom. Derek was still inside. I was just standing there, waiting for him, when an angel appeared! Somehow I mustered up the courage to speak to her.

I asked her name and if she'd like to smoke a joint. Her voice was so beautiful when she spoke, it gave me goosebumps. She told me her name was Sheri and that she'd love to, but she was waiting for a girlfriend to come out of the bathroom.

I said, "I am also waiting for a friend." The four of us walked behind a tree, I quickly rolled a joint, and we got high. Sheri became my lady for the next couple of years. Our relationship was strong, but the relationship I soon built with Sheri's father was even stronger.

*****

It's now Wednesday about 6:30 p.m. here on Delta Block. My Sara came for a visit at 5:30; it was nice to see her. We cried for a while, then talked about her trying to get a job at Olive Garden. I feel so bad making her grow up. I guess I didn't realize how much she depended on me. I love her and hope she does some good things for herself while I am down.

It's about 7:30 a.m. on Thursday morning. We had breakfast out in the pod, we do that every once in a while. I sat with William, William is a hard hitter who would like to come and work for me and help me collect some of the money owed to me. Of course, it takes me back to the question of "What do I want to do with the rest of my life?" If I step into the realm of recovery, then all the money owed to me will be forfeited, but maybe that's okay. Perhaps that's the cost of peace of mind. Sure is a bit of money, and I'm so broke. I guess Sara and I will have to decide, but we do need to get her off the dope and get her to stop using the heroin that she sells. If Sara keeps using the Black, then I'll want to keep shooting the go-fast, and that means I'll be back here in the grey bar hotel. I must stop!

*****

Clyde N., Sheri's dad, was in the business of moving large quantities of the green dope. He and his buddy, Wendell, would fill up large U-Haul trucks with hundreds of pounds of green buds in Tucson, Arizona, and drive them up to Salt Lake. We would wait for it to get dark then we would carry the pot in to Sheri and Clyde's apartment through the ground-level sliding glass door. There was so much pot in Clyde's room that there was no room for a bed, so he slept on the couch in the living room.

The best part about all this lime green bud was that Clyde would front me quarter pounds for $200 apiece. Now back in the eighties, pot sold for $15 an eighth of an ounce. So if I sold a quarter pound out in eighths, that came out to be $480. So owing two bills for it left me $280 profit per quarter pound. It would take me about three a day to move a quarter pound at school. Plus, I would sell full quarter pounds for $250 or half pounds for $500. I did this a couple of times a week.

Making money when I was fourteen and fifteen years old was very easy. I also bought and sold blotter acid and shrooms (psychedelic mushrooms). The mushrooms were a seasonal thing, but the acid was always available. I would trade my friend, Tim, a quarter pound of pot for a sheet (100 hits) of "Black Pyramid" acid. The acid always sold for $5 dollars a hit, so it was always a fast way of turning $200 into $500. I remember in the two hours before the Van Halen "1984" concert, I sold an entire sheet of acid standing outside the Salt Palace, just asking people if they wanted to trip.

Just before I turned sixteen, a big wave of ether-based cocaine flooded the Salt Lake valley. I thought I loved Sheri. I thought I loved my mom and my sisters. I also thought I loved the feeling of an orgasm and the taste of chocolate and the smell of freshly roasted coffee. I was wrong. I didn't know what true love was until Bob shot that ether-based cocaine in my fifteen-year-old arm for the first time! Bob was a bum or a freeloader. He hung out at Sheri and Clyde's apartment. He was an old friend of Clyde's. Bob was a jerk, but he knew how to shoot dope.

We were over at Clyde and Sheri's one day, and Bob told me he would shoot me up if I had some coke for him. So the day came when we were both there, and I had half a gram of cocaine. Bob got in to Clyde's cupboard and grabbed a ten-pack of needles. Clyde was diabetic, so he always had needles. Bob and I left Clyde's and hitchhiked to Bob's apartment. It was only about thirty blocks, so not too far. The feeling that rushed over me when that coke hit my heart was so exciting, and the tingle that went all the way down to my fingertips is indescribable. But what I remember most about that first shot was the taste; the absolute ether gag actually choked me. It was incredible, I've never felt so much love for anything before.

*****

It's Friday night, the eighteenth of April 2014. Tomorrow will be thirty days down, thirty days without Sara, thirty days with no tobacco, and thirty days without drugs. It's about 10:00 p.m.; today was commissary day, so I'm full. It's nice to have a full stomach when you go to sleep. You tend to sleep better. The jail doesn't want you to sleep well. They're afraid of people liking it here and not wanting to leave. For some, the idea of having three hot meals and a cot to sleep on works just fine for them. For me, I really missed my freedom and the taste of a cigarette.

The kind of life I was living was so fast, though that I never had a day off of work, ever! I was lucky if I got six straight hours of sleep without being woken by someone needing to be fixed. It was so easy to get back addicted to that power that comes from having the dope. Being a heroin dealer and a psych major went hand in hand for me; fixing people was what I did. It was all an illusion, though. I never really had any power or control. I was being manipulated just like the puppets on the dope. I thought I was doing good, making a name for myself. I was just being set up to get busted!

*****

I moved out from Derek's mom's place and was living with my mom and three of my sisters—Kimberly, Josie, Mia—and my mom's boyfriend Charles. My other sister, Kyra, was my dad and stepmom Patrica's daughter, so she lived with them. Kyra was just a couple years old when I moved out from my dad's. Life was very wild with lots of traffic in and out of my mom's condo, but that's who I was. So there were never any questions from my mom about the traffic, and I'm not sure why. Sheri and I were real bad drinkers. Our lives had become about getting drunk every night. I guess *"half measures availed us nothing."*

We were both somewhat attending Valley alternative high school. There was always a party every night at someone's house. Valley was in Sandy, by my dad's house, so I had a lot of old friends and friends of my big sisters that also attended. I went to Valley for a few years and must have made fifty thousand dollars selling drugs there, played lots of hacky sack but never earned a single high school credit.

One drunken night after leaving a keg party that a friend from Valley was throwing, Sheri and her friend, Kim, were with Bob and I. Bob and I thought it would be fun to go to the Denny's restaurant and dine-and-dash. That's where we would go in and pig out, then wait until our server was in the back, then run out and jump in the car and speed away. After our dine-and-dash was successful, we decided to run in the 7-Eleven and put a case of beer in each hand then run out. This also worked, so we did another and another. We had twelve twenty-four-packs of beer in the hatchback of Bob's little car.

It was getting late, and Sheri had to get home, so we dropped her off. On our way up to drop me off, we decided to do one more 7-Eleven. Bob parked on the road on the southside of the store, facing east. He and I went in and left Kim in the car. We had a hero working behind the counter. As Bob and I and the four cases of Budweiser and were leaving the store, this hero jumped over the counter and ran after us. We threw the beer in the back of the car and quickly jumped in. Bob threw the car in reverse and punched the gas. He must have been doing twenty-five miles per hour when he pushed down the clutch and went to second gear as he spun the wheel 180 degrees.

It was an awesome race car move, except for that damn telephone pole. Bob's car was sort of wrapped around that pole. The car hit the pole right at the driver's door. Bob's neck was mutilated, and I just hit my forehead on the rearview mirror. I knew the cops were coming, so I jumped out of the car and jumped into some nearby bushes as I watched Bob trying to unwedge his car from that pole by gunning it in reverse over and over. Finally, it broke loose, and Bob and Kim drove down the road. I jumped out of the bushes and started walking home.

After a few minutes, Bob and Kim pulled up next to me. As I was getting into Bob's car, Kim said, "Where's Sheri?"

I tried so hard to convince them both that we had dropped Sheri off prior to our last beer heist; neither of them could remember. The shock factor plus all the alcohol we had consumed made remembering anything quite a chore.

As we pulled into my mom's condo complex, I looked over at Bob. His neck was bleeding so bad that his shirt was soaking wet with blood. I knew I had to wake my mom up and get Bob to the hospital. I left Bob and Kim in the kitchen and I ran up the stairs in to my mom's room and switched on the light. I said, "Mom, we had a car accident, and Bob is downstairs bleeding badly. We need to take him to the hospital!"

She looked up at me from her bed and said, "Oh my God, what happened to your face? Are you okay?"

I walked over to the mirror to look see what she was talking about and I was a little shocked; not really shocked about seeing the dried blood starting from my forehead and ending at my chin, but shocked that neither Kim nor Bob told me what my face looked like before I woke my mother.

The seven stitches I received on my forehead were nothing compared to the ninety-three that Bob's neck needed. We learned at the hospital that whenever there is a car accident with injury, the police must be called. When the cop arrived, he said he wasn't real surprised to see us. He said that they received four calls from 7-Elevens about the "Beer Bandits."

I said, "Sir, I don't know what you're talking about!" But when the tow truck and the police showed up over at my mom's and saw the sixteen twenty-four-packs of beer in Bob's car, they knew I was full of shit; beer and shit that is! Bob stayed at the hospital, and I was too young to go to jail, so they let Kim and I leave with my mom. Kim stayed over with me at my mom's condo. She had no real injuries, but was very shaken up.

Sheri and I would always break up every now and then, but we would always end up back together. One night, Sheri, Phil, Bart, Kim, and I were partying at some guy's house in the Holladay area. That was the area where I lived. Sheri and I got into one of our drunken "shouting at each other" fights. We were all outside by the car when Sheri pushed me and my foot hit the curb, and down I went. The four of them jumped in Bart's car, and they drove off. I walked about half a mile home and passed out.

The next morning when I came to, I called Sheri's apartment with no answer. I figured she and Kim slept over at Wendy's apartment downtown. Wendy didn't have a phone. It was Sunday, so there were no buses, so I hitchhiked downtown. When I got there, she told me that she hadn't seen Sheri nor Kim. I proceeded to hitchhike out to Sandy where Phil lived. I didn't know where Kim or Bart lived, so it was my only hope. When I got to Sandy and was approaching Phil's apartment, I got a sick, kind of scared feeling inside me. I didn't even knock on the door. I just walked in, and as I approached Phil's bedroom door, his roommate said, "He's not alone." When I walked into Phil's bedroom and saw him and Sheri lying naked on his bed, something inside me broke. It's been over thirty years now, and I still can't fix it. I guess the truly broken heart can never mend. I do remember having sex a number of times with Sheri after that, but it was never the same.

My mornings were always the worst. I would come to or wake up and have no memory of how I got home or even where I was the night before. But I always had a feeling of regret in my gut. A few hours later, the phone would start to ring, and my questions about me and my actions the night before were soon answered. It would always start with a laugh and usually the same kind of comments and questions like, "I can't believe how much you drank last night!" Then, "Did you stay until the second keg was kissed?" One of my favorite comments was, "I can't believe you took that ugly girl home with you last night. Is she still there?"

It was the wrongs that I did to people that I would start remembering first and the lies I would tell just to make me look better to others. I would hate myself every morning and I would always try to fix the remorse with a couple bong hits, but it never helped it; it just kind of helped me forget why I hated myself, but the hate was still there. There was something amazing that happened to me every day about 4:00 p.m. I'd be down at the school or doing a deal somewhere, it didn't really matter where I was. But the same thought came in my head every day, and that thought was, *I'll do it different tonight, I won't drink as much, I can do it right!* But after I started drinking, I was not able to stop, ever!

When I was sixteen, I met Barbie. She also attended Valley High School. Barbie drove a white Chevy Camaro. The car was beautiful, almost as beautiful as her. I was in love once again, with her not the car—well, maybe both—and I just couldn't get enough of her. I became so obsessed with Barbie that I no longer cared about working things out with Sheri. Barbie's father, Francis, was a urologist at a local hospital, and her mom, Barbara, was a stay-at-home mom. Three months after I started seeing Barbie, I moved her out of her parents' house and in with me. We lived a in a couple of different places over the next year. The first place was in my friends' place, Clyde and Joe's basement. We threw kegs every weekend, and I kept selling my drugs. I met a guy named Tino who introduced me to a water-soluble pill called Dilaudid. He told me it was synthetic heroin. I only shot it one time because it felt so good. It made me feel like the world was perfect and everything was right. I knew if I kept shooting it, I'd be hooked forever!

In February of 1987, Barbie and I got pregnant. The first part of March, Barbie told me she was late, and she was always quite regular with her cycle. So she made a doctor's appointment with her gynecologist. Those appointment were always free for her because her doctor was friends with her dad. Sure enough, we were pregnant, a little scared, but a lot excited. So in March, we moved in with my mom and family. I officially dropped out of school, not that my teachers would notice anyway.

I now was committed to working a real job where I would pay taxes because I was going to be a father. I did realize that I would have no way to pay for any of the pregnancy; thank God for the relationship between her doctor and her dad. I was committed to doing all I could. Barbie and I were so excited about being parents. We were both only seventeen but were sure we could do it. We both felt so sure that Barbie was carrying a baby girl that we named her Teddy. When Barbie was just a few weeks along, I would talk to Teddy every day.

My grandfather started painting the numbers on the airplanes in WW2. He brought his painting skills home with him and had a big painting company here in Salt Lake City. I learned to paint when I was quite young. Being the first part of March, it was too cold for there to be much work as a painter. So I learned how to cook chicken for the colonel at KFC. My pot sales were still at a steady pace. I was bringing in about $500 profit every week. My shooting cocaine was down to only a couple times a month.

Barbie and I were good friends with Olivia and Swidey. They were rock stars. When I was living with my dad, I sometimes would hang out with a friend named Guy. Now Guy was a party animal and lived pretty close to my dad's house. Guy's big brother, Charles, was in a band called A.Z.R.O. Charles was a rhythm guitarist, and Swidey was the lead guitarist. That was back in the first part of the eighties.

In 1987, Swidey was playing in a band called MEGATACK, and his girlfriend Olivia was on vocals. On Friday, the thirteenth of March, Barbie and I were at MEGATACK's band practice. Swidey asked me if I wanted to run to the store with him for more beers. Of course, I agreed. We pulled out of the Midvale Storage center where the practice studio was. Swidey was driving Parish's car. Parish was the other guitarist. I was sitting passenger. As soon as we pulled out onto Allen Street, a cop turned his lights on to pull us over. Swidey turned to me and said, "Darren, I don't have a license, please switch seats with me."

Now this was Swidey. He was such an awesome guitar player like Randy Rhodes, Eric Clapton, or even the great Jimmy Hendrix. There was no way I could turn his request down. The only problem was that I was sloppy drunk. The cop was Sergeant Pepper working for the Midvale Police, who was actually quite cool. When he approached the window, he said, "I saw you switch seats, but you're in the driver's seat now, so you get out and do a sobriety test for me." I think he could smell the alcohol on me.

After miserably failing the sobriety test, I was cuffed and taken to the police station. He sat me down at a desk, uncuffed me, then grabbed a hard-plastic straw-shaped device that was hooked on a tube connected to a machine, handed it to me, and said, "Blow in this." I blew into the straw-shaped device for what seemed like forever. The tube was then taken out of my mouth by Sergeant Pepper. He then pressed a button on the machine, and I heard a long beep, and he said, "Sorry, didn't work. Do it again."

I then stood up and said, "Fuck you, you think I'm fucked up. I think your machine is fucked up!"

He then informed me that with a DUI, I would lose my license for ninety days, but if I refused the test, I would lose my license for a full year. I acknowledged that I had heard him, and then he said to me, "When the letter gets to your house, you can't drive a car for one full year." I was too young to go to jail, so that nice cop dropped me off at Barbie's dad's apartment, which was pretty close.

Six days later on the nineteenth of March, Barbie and I went to an Alice Cooper concert. It was "The Nightmare Returns" tour. I got so drunk before the show, so she drove. Like most the concerts I attended, I don't remember most of them.

A month and a half later, on the twenty-fifth of April, there was still no letters sent to my house stating that I couldn't drive. So when Trevor called at 8:00 a.m. and said, "I've a fifth of Crown Royal and two tickets for all-day skiing up at Snowbird," I knew my mom would let me borrow her car. A week before, I had gotten a new job painting houses because it was now spring, so I had stopped cooking chicken for the colonel. Now I had worked six days and got the seventh day off. Barbie was a little over two months pregnant, and she wanted to spend my first day off shopping for baby clothes. That was the plan, but when Trevor and his bottle called with two tickets to the Bird, I guess the plan changed.

I don't recall anything at all about that day, the twenty-fifth of April 1987. The doctors told me one day I might remember that day, but it's been twenty-seven years now, and I still don't.

From what I've been told, Trevor and I started drinking first thing that morning. We drank hard and skied hard all day. The ski lifts closed down at 4:30, so we started our slow drive down the crowded canyon. We were smoking some pot in a bent-up Budweiser can with holes poked in it. I know this because my family left it in the car, which they let me see one year later. While driving down the canyon, we came to a stretch of road called "Seven Sisters." It is a short straightaway, so of course I pulled in to the left oncoming lane, trying to pass a few of the cars in front of me. Thank God one of the cars I passed was a surgeon from Snowbird. As I was passing these slow-moving cars, I went too far left, and the car caught loose gravel. I must have overcorrected, and the car went into a spin across the road, back over to the right side, then off the right side, and I proceeded to roll my mom's car three times, front end over back end. We were traveling down the canyon, so the mountain was on the right side of the road. The front end hit first, and the inertia caused the back end to come up over the front, and the rolling began. Trevor's seat broke, and he fell in to the backseat where he remained for all three rolls. When the car stopped rolling, he was able to climb out through the shattered back window. Trevor didn't know his name or my name. He was in massive shock but physically was not hurt; I wasn't so fortunate.

    The first time the front end of the car hit the mountain, I shattered my nose completely on the front window. As my left lung started filling with blood, the flipping of the car pulled me back and to the left toward the driver's door. The back right side of my head bent the frame of the door out about a foot and a half; my body followed my head out of the car, and I rolled down the side of the mountain back to the road. By the grace of God, the surgeon who I had passed while racing down the canyon actually watched the accident happen. He was able to pull his car over right by where I landed. When he put his hands on my chest, he could tell I was not breathing. He did declare me dead but then got a respirator out of his car and put it on my face. He was able to tell that my left lung was full of blood and unable to hold air but my right lung was able too. He then called on his radio for the AirMed helicopter to fly in to the canyon and pick me up. I was then flown to the University of Utah Medical Center where I was in a coma and unable to breathe on my own. My family was called.

Nineteen days later, I came out of my coma. My mom later told me that nurses would come in every hour and turn me on my stomach, then beat on my back, trying to help me cough that blood up out of my lung. Once I was out of my coma, I was transferred to LDS hospital. My lung had still too much blood in it to be driven, so a Life Flight helicopter flew up from LDS hospital, picked me up, and flew me back to LDS in downtown Salt Lake City. I was in that second hospital for only fourteen days. For some reason, I insisted on curling my left arm up. The problem was all the tubes that I still had in the arm. So the nurses had to strap my arms down. Having the blood in my lung for that much time caused me to get pneumonia so bad that it almost killed me.

When I was in this hospital, my family put headphones on my ears with the music just blasting way loud. I guess they were trying to wake me up. Barbie and I had a song together by Alice Cooper. It was on his "Welcome to My Nightmare" album. The song was called "Only Women Bleed." When that song started playing, I spoke for the first time. Actually, my family says I yelled, "Turn it down!" I haven't any memory of either of those first two hospitals.

My first memory of anything was when I was being loaded in to the ambulance to go to my third and final hospital. This happened at the end of May 1987, and my mother rode with me in the back of the ambulance from LDS hospital in Salt Lake City to McKay Dee hospital in Ogden, Utah. I was very fortunate that Ogden was only about thirty miles north of Salt Lake because in the basement of McKay Dee hospital was Stewart Rehab.

Back in the eighties, Stewart Rehab was known as one of the best rehabilitation clinics on the west side of the country. The entire trip to Ogden from Salt Lake seemed like it took about two minutes. I was still slipping in and out of consciousness; my lung did fine.

I lived on the fifth floor of McKay Dee hospital for about a month and a half. My doctors were Dr. Thomas and Dr. Black. I remember Barbie always being there at first. Even when I'd wake up in the night, she'd be there. I guess once I got stable, they no longer let her stay overnight with me. I had the biggest fear of being locked up, and I don't know where that came from. My doctors didn't know either, but they ensured me that because of my "major head injury," I would never be incarcerated. I guess eventually I believed them because the fear went away. I took physical therapy twice a day.

My physical therapist's name was Heidi. Heidi would hold me up as I would walk through this contraption that had two parallel waist-high bars. We would just go back and forth until I got too tired to stand. That happened real fast at first, but as time when on, I got a little stronger. Judy was my occupational therapist. I met with her twice a day as well. Judy would have me do fun things like puzzles and working with beads and putting the beads on a wire. Then she would wheel me up to my room and teach me how to get dressed. My speech therapist and I met three times a day, five days a week, for six weeks. Her name was Stephanie. Stephanie was the nicest lady, but speech therapy was the hardest therapy I had. I could not get the sounds out of my throat. It was so frustrating. I couldn't speak at all for about five or six weeks after the accident. My vocal cords were paralyzed and probably will always be partially paralyzed. As the years have gone by, my voice, when I get enough sleep, has become easier to understand.

The last couple weekends in my third hospital, they let me leave with my mom and sisters. We would drive to our house in Salt Lake City. On the weekend, the drive home took about twenty-five minutes. After being on a catheter for the couple months that I was, and the way the car rocked, I could travel about halfway home before I'd had to pull out a plastic bottle called a urinal and fill it up. The drive from where we lived in Salt Lake to the hospital in Ogden during rush hour traffic took my mom about forty minutes. She drove up to see me every day I was there. I have the best mom in the world.

Because there were a couple months that I have no memory of, I asked the people that were in my life to write a bit about that time.

My little sister Josie wrote a paper about how she remembered my accident called "Coming to Terms:"

> When we drove up to the house, the garage door was open and the car was gone. I knew instantly that something was wrong. Why would they leave the garage door open, especially when it was one of the cardinal sins at our house? We walked into the basement, and all of the lights were on and the TV was blaring. We looked at each other in wonder. Where were my brother and older sister? In silent agreement, my mother, my younger sister, and I walked upstairs in hopes they would be in the kitchen or living room.
>
> As we reached the top of the steep staircase, the phone rang. We stopped dead in our tracks and looked at each other, then at the phone, and back at each other. My mother picked up the phone, and a look of intense concentration came over her face and was quickly transformed into a look of horror. She told someone on the other end that she would be right there. When she hung up the phone, she said in a quavering voice, "There's been an accident and Darren is in the hospital. They don't know if he'll make it."
>
> I was the first one to go downstairs and get in the car. My father was still in the garage, grumbling about the garage being left open. I told him that my brother had been in an accident. He mentioned something about how now the car was probably totaled, and I automatically assumed he was more worried about the car than his stepson. Looking back, I realize that is the way he deals with things by quietly focusing on another issue, one that is tangible, one that he can deal with, not the one he has no control over.

The eight-minute ride to the University Hospital took an eternity. I looked at everyone in the car and wondered what was going through their minds. I was afraid for my mom. If she lost her only son, she would die inside. How would we survive if that happened? When I glanced at my little sister, I was curious if she was thinking the same things I was or if she was really scared. I was in too much shock to be scared.

This could not be happening to my brother, to my family. Things like this only happen to other people. How could it be possible that my cocky seventeen-year-old brother was lying in the hospital, holding on for dear life? I had just seen him that morning, getting ready to go skiing on the last ski day of the year. He was full of life as he ate his cereal, "hyper" and excited, joking around with us and being playful. As he jumped up to leave, he kissed and hugged my mom good-bye and told her he loved her. She reminded him to wear his seatbelt, and off he went to dare the black diamond slopes of Snowbird.

Now I was on the way to the hospital in a never-ending car ride with a deafening silence around me. Finally, we pulled up to the hospital, and my memories skip to finding my older sister and my brother's girlfriend in a long stark white hallway which reeked of unknown chemicals. My sister poured out all the details she knew in a rush of jumbled words, the words I have since repeated a million times to anyone who has asked about my brother.

He had been driving back from Snowbird after sneaking into the bar and having a drink and after having a few hits of whatever else was available. He was doing fine until he got behind a car that was going too slow. He passed the car in a no-passing zone and overcorrected when he went back to his lane and hit the side of the mountain. The car flipped the opposite direction and rolled three times. His best friend stayed in the car, stopped by the skis in between their seats. My brother was not so lucky.

He flew out the driver's side window, tumbled down the hillside, crashing his head on the rocks. A moment later, his friend crawled safely out of the car and wandered around to find Darren. By a strange twist of fate, the car behind Darren was filled with doctors coming from a convention. They got their bags and went to Darren. When they found him, they thought he was dead. Somehow, the hospital was contacted, and a helicopter came and took him away.

Five hours later, when we arrived at the hospital, Darren was in intensive care on a breathing machine with not much chance of surviving. They let us in to see him. He was lying on a tall white bed surrounded by a curtain, which was open. He had blood in his hair, a gash on his eye and head, and his nose looked broken. There was this awful blue thing in his mouth which was hooked up to a large respirator. It made an unnatural sucking noise.

When I picked up Darren's hand to hold and reassure myself that he was alive, I noticed the rocks, dirt, and blood under his fingernails, and for the first time, I wondered at the terror he must have felt flying through the air, crashing to the ground, and grasping to the side of the mountain before he fell unconscious. The sight of him in the hospital is vivid in my mind today, nearly nine years later.

That night, we all slept in the hospital waiting room on the floor, trying to comfort each other but not really knowing how. It didn't seem real, and there was nothing we could do, so we just tried to stay sane. I remember going downstairs to the cafeteria in the basement to get something to eat with my brother's girlfriend and my younger sister. My brother's girlfriend was a few months pregnant and had cravings constantly. We stopped at a soda machine, and she mentioned how she had a paper cut and it really hurt. We looked at each other and burst out laughing. The irony was too much for us, and we laughed for a long time, letting go of our emotions until we began crying.

My brother's girlfriend had one wish that night. She wished that if Darren woke up, his first words would be to ask for her. She was only seventeen. I thought it very romantic but secretly wished he would ask for my mom. Sometime during that endless night, we found out that he had brain damage and might need a pancreas transplant. I had no idea what it meant to have brain damage, but I had seen coma patients on TV, so when the doctors told us he was in a coma, I figured he would wake up and be fine.

Sometime around the second day, the hospital moved him to his own room and imposed visiting regulations on us. Only family could visit, one member at a time for ten minutes, every hour on the hour. Over the next few weeks, I remember bits and pieces of some of my visits vividly.

The room had a strong odor, which sends me into instant flashbacks whenever I come across it. I would go in and stand by his bed, pick up his hand, and talk to him. I would tell him everything would be okay if he would just wake up. We really needed him. I would fill him in on my day at school or the growth of his unborn child. It was chatter to keep myself going, to maybe keep him going. We have always had an up-and-down relationship, and he had always been somewhat of a brat. Nothing changed when he was in a coma.

I was feeling really sad and worried one day after school. I was sitting next to him, crying, and all of a sudden, I felt something wet on my leg. I instantly jumped up and saw that he had relieved himself in the bed. I then realized he must have pulled out his catheter. This seemed to be a sign that he knew I was sitting next to him and he thought I needed a good laugh or a reality check. Every so often, he would squeeze my hand really hard, and I believed this meant he could hear me. The nurses said it was his reflexes, but I needed to believe otherwise.

The thought that most crossed my mind in our quiet ten-minute sessions together was the fact that it only took him a fraction of a second to make the mistake that got him here. I could never accept the fact that he might die, but I was not prepared for the months he would have to spend in the hospital or for the responsibilities I would have when he came home.

I have so many memories of the hospital, the people who came to visit, the conversations, the effect of all this on my mother, my brother's daily status, and the overall chaotic emotions of all involved. Picking just a few to write seems impossible.

I am not sure why I am writing this nine years after it happened. Maybe it was just time to see it on paper, to relive one of my most life-changing experiences. Perhaps it is because I have not come to terms with any of it. I do know that my brother's accident taught me to live life to its fullest and to appreciate all that I have. Someday, I will be able to lay this story to rest, to not cry when I tell it, to forgive my brother for creating it. But I cannot forget it nor change it. His accident, in a way, will last forever in my life as well as his. It is part of my memory and has changed me.

My little sister, Mia, wrote:

The Day that Changed Our Family Forever

I remember the day of my older brother's accident so vividly in so many ways, yet there are pieces of that day that I can't recall at all. Although I was only thirteen years old at the time, it was a day that I will never forget, a day that forever changed our lives—the most traumatic experience of my life to date.

My mom, stepdad, older sister, Josie, and I had spent the day in Ogden, getting our hair done and visiting family. When we arrived home that evening, the phone was ringing, and my mom ran to answer it. I don't recall who it was on the other end of the line; I just recall the panic on my mom's face as she listened. Her first response was, "With the car?"

When she finally hung up, she told us Darren had been in an accident and that he was in the hospital and we needed to get there right away!

I don't remember much until the moment we got to the hospital and my oldest sister, Kimberly, came rushing out to us in hysterics. Not only had her brother and best friend been hurt, but her boyfriend was in the car as well. Trevor's fate had been much luckier than my brother's. He survived the accident with only minor cuts and bruises. My brother, on the other hand, was in intensive care on life support.

I will never forget the anguish that my mom was experiencing, the hysterical sobbing and complete utter breakdown that her baby boy and only son was fighting for his life. To this day, I can still picture that moment of the complete despair my mom felt. We were all devastated and heartbroken, but at that time, I didn't understand the magnitude of what it would be like as a parent to see your child in a critical state. I understand that now as a mother of two boys, and my heart breaks for my mom on that day and the many long days ahead.

When we got to the ICU to see him, he was barely recognizable, bruised, swollen, cut, and he was hooked up to so many machines. He wasn't breathing on his own, and I can still hear the sound of the respirator fighting to keep him alive. We were told he had a severe head injury and was in a coma. If he did make it out of the coma, it would be a long recovery.

I had always worried something would happen to my brother. I knew that he as a big partier and involved in drugs and alcohol. I remember crying myself to sleep when I was only in fifth grade because I thought he was going to die. This was my worst nightmare.

I remember sleeping at the hospital those first couple of nights, not wanting to leave my mom. She was still in such inconsolable despair. She basically lived at the hospital for the first few weeks.

The days leading up to when he started becoming responsive are foggy, but I do recall praying every moment that I had the chance that he would wake up and be okay. I didn't know how any of us, especially my mom, would survive if he didn't.

My mom was my best friend and such a huge part of my life. It was so hard not having her at home every day while we tried to go on with our lives, go to school, and be normal teens. I had a hard time staying focused in school in the beginning. I found myself often looking fondly at my friends with envy at their "normal lives."

After what seemed like weeks, my brother, still in a coma, started to respond. Bit by bit, piece by piece, he started squeezing our hands, responding to our voices, and slowly fluttering his eyelids. Waking up from a coma is nothing like it plays out on TV where suddenly the person wakes up and is fine. The longer you are in coma, the more brain cells start to die and the longer recovery or even potential for non-recovery. It was a waiting game, and we had no idea what would happen if he did come out of it.

Ten days—that is the amount of time he was in a coma before he was responsive. Ten days that felt like ten months just waiting for my "big brother" to be okay. Being the youngest of the family, he was always so sweet to me. I was his little "Leapchun," and the thought of losing him was unimaginable.

The doctors told us that the part of his brain that tells us to walk and talk was severely damaged and that he would have to learn all of those skills again. At the young age of seventeen, my big, strong, macho older brother had to learn basic motor skills all over again. It was an absolute miracle that he survived but heartbreaking, knowing the long road he had ahead.

After he woke up, he was then transferred to LDS hospital for rehab and finally to MacKay Dee in Ogden where he would spend months in rehabilitation. Ogden was a good forty-five-minute drive from our home, a drive that my mom made every night after she had worked a full day, just to be with her son. I can remember driving up with her often or as often as you could expect from a thirteen-year-old. The drive back home at 9:00 or 10:00 p.m. on a weeknight was tough on my mom. She used to ask me to talk to her to keep her awake when she felt sleepy. I remember just wanting to be with her and support her as much as I could.

My brother was making progress every day. Slowly, he was able to start putting words into sentences. Step by step, he began to walk with a walker. From what I can recall, he was usually in good spirits in spite of everything. Yet, the brother that I knew before the accident was a much different person now, which is expected with a traumatic brain injury.

It was summertime when he was finally ready to come home and continue rehab. My older sister, Josie, and I were out of school for the summer, so we began helping him when my mom was at work. We would do his stretches with him and help in any way we could. I can't recall the exact timeline as to when he was able to walk again and speak with more ease, but I am sure that for my dear brother, it had to have felt like an eternity.

The day Darren was in his accident was the worst day of our family's lives. It changed us forever, and it also made us stronger. We have been through a lot together as a family and we couldn't have done it without our mom's strength and dedication.

I have so much gratitude that my brother is alive. The amount of trauma and pain that he has endured is more than most people ever have to go through in a lifetime. Yet, he never complains that he can't walk as fast or speak as clearly as many others. He lives his life with compassion and perseverance, and I am so lucky to call this amazing human being my brother. I love you, big brother, and I look up to you more than you can ever imagine.

My stepmother, Patrica, wrote:

We got the call about Darren, and I remember running out of the house to make it up to the University of Utah Hospital. When we were walking into the ICU, I remember his feet. They were still and looked cold. It took my breath away and brought on the tears and fear that we were too late. It didn't look like there was any life in his body, just the machines that took over his breathing. The ten-minute visits seemed short.

I remember waiting till it was our turn to spend a few minutes with him and then not knowing what to say to his tender but bludgeoned face. His hands were warm and gave relief that he was alive. The sounds of the machines to help him breath were a stark reality. I was grateful for the medical help.

During his time in the coma, Gary got a call in the middle of the night from Darren. They talked like nothing had happened; it was cordial and greetings of "Hi, Dad" and "How are you?"

Gary told me it was Darren on the phone. Darren was clear in his speech. We looked at each other, surprised and excited that he was out of his coma. The next day, we found out he was still in the coma. It was a strange and blessed event. We're still trying to figure it out. News of a brain stem injury started to be shared around the family. I didn't know the details of how it would affect his life. I knew there would be physical therapy that could help and a lot of hard work on his part. The accident has become a pivotal point in his timeline.

My dad, Gary, wrote:

> I saw him awake. I have never had a chronicle memory. My mother does. Any gene contributing to Darren's superb one was latent in me. So not knowing the order of things, I'll try some.
>
> One day, I walked unaccompanied into his room and found his eyes open. I approached and greeted him. He responded normally. "Nurse! He's awake!" I yelled (can't remember what happened after the visit to the lookout at LDS). I remember while visiting him at LDS Hospital an occasion wherein a friend of his and I took him in a wheelchair to a place where he could be in the sun for a while. He was in his all too famil-

iar breathing sack-o'-bones condition. His friend had a "Big Gulp"-type drink with him.

During the trip, Darren raised himself upright and asked his friend, "Whatcha drinkin'? Can I have a swig?" Whereupon Darren reached and grasped the container, took some generous swallows, and returned the drink, saying, "Thank you," then returned it to him.

There was a call from McKay Dee Hospital shortly after he was transferred to McKay Dee Hospital in Ogden where I visited him and witnessed his usual incapacity, comatose; he called me in the middle of the night. His voice was clear, his demeanor calm, speech lucid and aware. We discussed how he was feeling and how he got the phone in his hand. He said, "There's one right here on the wall next to my bed, so I just picked it up and dialed" (I've been in the hospital much lately and rarely could figure how to get an outside line).

We talked about other things for another minute or two. I wasn't able to think of things to say as I was under the influence of Trazadone, and I was somewhat speechless, being astounded by what was happening. Patrica, having heard my side of the conversation and not quite believing what she witnessed (for I had addressed him as Darren frequently), asked "Who was that?"

Within a day or so later, I went excitedly to see him and was quite surprised to find him with no more capacity than he had before that startling night. But I still had more hope because of that night.

"I can walk if the wind isn't blowing too hard." I remember him saying that to someone in his early new life. Working with his disappearing heels, it was sad to see his heels disappearing into his lower legs and feet. During my visits, I always used some time in trying to stretch his calves.

Old friends found him after he had returned home. His old friends started gathering around. I was frightened that his physical problems would be dwarfed by his old friends, some of which were people.

My mother, Phoebe, wrote:

> On April 25, 1987, I, two of my daughters, Josie and Mia, and my significant other, Charles, went to Ogden Utah for the day. It was a Saturday, and I was getting my hair cut and colored. We returned home early evening to our Holladay home to find the garage open, car missing, and the lights in the house and TV on! Strange! I had loaned my car to my son to go skiing with a friend but knew he would have the car back by then.
>
> The phone was ringing as we entered. It was the University of Utah Hospital telling us that Darren had been in a car accident and that we needed to come now! My mind was racing, hoping for the best but afraid of the worst. The four of us were mostly silent driving to the hospital. As we entered the emergency room, we were greeted by my oldest daughter, Kimberly, and Darren's girlfriend, Barbie. They were both crying, and when Kimberly saw me, she started sobbing.
>
> I saw Darren lifeless on the bed and the sound of a respirator breathing for him. He was so pale. His face looked plastic. His hair was wet and pulled back from his forehead, and there was a large gaping hole above his eye that needed to be

stitched. He still had some blood in his hair, and his knuckles were raw like he had scraped them on impact. I couldn't believe this was happening! We were not given a lot of information about his condition. They had determined his neck wasn't broken, only his nose. They were keeping him in a coma due to the amount of pain he would be experiencing.

They were telling us he might be awake in the morning and were going to do a brain scan. I wanted and hoped and prayed like never before that I would see him awake in the morning, but I was very afraid. I couldn't grasp what might be happening to all of us and especially my son. I can't remember when I started crying that night or when I stopped. They moved him to ICU. I wasn't leaving him alone at the hospital. They had a large waiting room for ICU patients with large recliners. All the girls stayed with me.

The car accident happened after Darren and his friend, Trevor, had finished spending the day skiing and drinking at Snowbird. He was nearing the Seven Sisters Turns when he became impatient with the slowness of the single-lane traffic and passed a car. He swung out too far and hit the gravel, overcorrected, and rolled the car several times. They weren't wearing seat belts, and he went out the driver's side rolled up window. Trevor was fortunate enough to be thrown into the backseat.

There was, fortunately, an emergency doctor a couple of cars behind that saw the accident. When he got to Darren lying on the ground, he was unresponsive. Blood had been running down his throat into his lungs. He was able to get him breathing, and Darren was life-flighted to the

University of Utah Hospital. The next morning, the reality hit that he was in a coma. They had done a scan and determined he had brain stem damage! They didn't need to do surgery at this point because even though his brain was swelling, he had extra space, so it was a waiting game to see what would happen in the next few days.

They also discovered due to blunt trauma to the pancreas that it was not functioning properly. The next few days are a blur. My normal life stopped! I was at the hospital, day and night, and barely left to go home to shower. We were told to talk to him about current events happening. The nurses told us there was no way to know but he might be able to hear us. We played music he loved and encouraged anyone who came to visit to talk to him. He developed pneumonia, and they had to prop him up to perform treatments on him. They inserted a suction tube down his throat often to clear the mucous because he was unable to cough.

Even though we were taking extra precautions when coming to ICU, he still had developed pneumonia. We had to wear gowns and face masks and wash our hands often. He slowly started to open his eyes and respond to our voices. He was unable to speak, but we knew he could hear us! What a relief.

His pancreas began functioning again. That was a relief that he wouldn't need surgery. For me and my family, our world as we knew it had stopped! My boss was understanding when I didn't return to work. I spent all my time at the hospital. After a few weeks in ICU, he had responded to treatment and was no longer in a coma. He was transported to LDS Hospital by

Life-Flight helicopter on May 13. As soon as he was transported to LDS Hospital, he became more alert. He responded to us with fingers for yes/no or very quiet whispers! He was able to stand with maximal assistance of two people for approximately five minutes.

They stapled a feeding tube to the side of his nose because he was unable to swallow food yet. The tube bothered him, and he regularly pulled it out! Rehab treatments started immediately. Physical therapy and speech therapy came and evaluated him so they could start the long process of teaching him to speak and walk. They told us that he might never be able to walk! How could this be? Less than a month earlier, my seventeen-year-old son was skiing, dancing, and now in an instant, his life was changed, and full recovery was looking grim!

Nine days later, on May 22, he was transported by ambulance to Stewart Rehabilitation Center in Ogden, Utah. It was about fifty miles from our home. The first thing he remembers of having been in an accident was in the ambulance on his way to Ogden. He would spend the next two months in intense therapy of every kind. They tested every avenue of cognitive, his word recognition, comprehension, and retention. The same with math skills, but each time he was tested, he had improved. The same with his speech therapy: Simple words with emphasis on volume. His diaphragm was weakened during the accident, and he struggled to push enough air out to be heard. He has struggled his entire life to speak loud enough to be heard.

Physical therapy was the most difficult of all. He had therapy three times a day. His progress was slow but steady. His hamstrings tightened as a result of being in a coma. Occupational therapy worked with him to relearn basic kitchen skills like getting utensils out of a drawer and making toast in his wheelchair. He had a significant tremor in his left arm, making any task a challenge. Dressing himself was a long process, but he was determined.

I wasn't with him during his therapy sessions. I would drive fifty miles every day after work and spend a few hours with him. He still had the feeding tube. When he tried to eat, he would choke. He kept saying hamburger, so he was definitely missing real food. One day, after they had taken his feeding tube out, I found him in the cafeteria for patients a short distance from his room. He was sitting at a table in his wheelchair. He was struggling to get food on his spoon and into his mouth. I became so emotional I couldn't let him see me cry, so I walked away. I knew he was progressing, but the reality of how far away he was from the wild and crazy teenager he was the day before the accident disturbed me.

Each day, he made tiny steps progressing. We were encouraged by his ability to slowly make cognitive connections. There is no way to know when the brain is shaken violently, where the damage will be, and what cells have been destroyed. Before his therapists were ready to release him, the insurance was running out! We met with his doctor, psychiatrist, and all his therapists and came up with a plan. Each day, he had multiple therapy sessions, so they decided to break it down to one session per day.

He was released from Stewart Rehab on July 17, 1987! I had wondered if he'd ever return again! He and I returned every day for a therapy session for two months. When he was home, he had to do therapy too. During the days, his sisters helped him exercise. They had to stand behind him as he struggled up each stair. They encouraged him to crawl for coordination and strength. He was required to do small motor skills also, like pick up Cheerios and do puzzles. We kept his wheelchair downstairs, so when he was upstairs, he had to figure out how to move around.

Slowly, with therapy at the rehab and at home, he was getting stronger and more coordinated. By the end of summer, it was determined that he should be returning to high school. His therapists and psychologist met with the appropriate school authorities to make a plan for him. He started at Cottonwood High School in January of 1988. The school bus picked him up in his wheelchair.

The story doesn't end here. Darren's struggles didn't end in the fall of 1987. His disabilities didn't. He's had to learn to live with them daily. This story is happening to families everywhere, every day. Bad choices can impact the lives of not only the chooser but the entire family for years to come! My hopes in writing this personal story is that if it makes at least one person stop and think before drinking or using or any number of other bad decisions, the tragedy that happened to Darren and his family will not have been in vain!

On the thirtieth of October 1987, a letter was requested from the Disability Determination Services. Dr. Thomas wrote:

> Darren was a seventeen-year-old who was involved in a one-car rollover on 4/25/87. He was

initially taken to the University of Utah Medical Center where his coma scale was between 3–5. An initial CT of the head revealed a hemorrhage of about 7–10 mm diameter in the right parietal area and evidence of blood in the left posterior occipital horn. A repeat CT scan one day later revealed similar findings.

While at the University Hospital, he developed a pulmonary infection attributed to aspiration. He also developed hyperamylasemia felt secondary to blunt trauma to the pancreas. He was, prior to transfer to our rehab center, able to stand with maximal assistance of two people for approximately five minutes and was able to respond with fingers for yes/no responses and some very quiet whispers.

He was admitted to the Stewart Rehabilitation Center on May 27, 1987. At the time of his admission, he could track visually in all directions. He made no verbalizations on my initial examination. Deep tendon reflexes were 2+ in the left upper extremity, 2=3+ in both lower extremities, and 1+ in the right upper extremity. He denied any difference in pinprick sensation from side to side. He had very weak knee extension bilaterally and minimal active hip flexion bilaterally. He had minimal movement of the left upper extremity and tended to hold it in a flexed position.

By the time of discharge on July 17, 1987, he was walking independently with the use of a walker. He continued to have difficulties with judgment and problem-solving abilities and required supervision in transfers and the activities of daily living. He was talking in short but appropriate sentences for simple questions. Our last evaluation conference with all of the therapists

> revealed the following: he was working in occupational therapy for about forty-five minutes per session and able to concentrate on tasks during that period quite well. He continues to have a rather pronounced tremor in the left extremity. He has figured out to position his arm in such a way to reduce the tremor so he can work on such things as small models. He is now working on moderate to high-level abstract reasoning, problem-solving, and judgment with about 85 percent accuracy in these three areas. Speech intelligibility is now at approximately 85 percent in normal conversation. He is requiring minimal assistance to ambulate sixty feet with a straight cane. He continues to require the assistance of a cane or some person to help him stand quietly.
>
> He does have a tremor in the lower extremities, especially noted on the left. He continues to use a wheelchair for distance ambulation or if he should have to stand quietly for any period of time.

I got out of McKay Dee hospital on the seventeenth of July, a couple weeks after I turned eighteen. My doctor, for my birthday, let Barbie spend the night with me. A lot of my body didn't seem to work any longer, but some of it worked just fine. The next sixteen months, I was in a wheelchair most of the time. I would get around the house on my hands and knees, crawling. I had killed all the brain cells that helped me have balance; my equilibrium was gone. Crawling worked because my head was so close to the ground. I only stayed sober for about a week after I got out; I did this for my mom.

When I got home from the hospital, I had the same friends, went to the same places, and did the same things. With my bladder the way it was, I had to ask someone to wheel me to the bathroom every fifteen minutes. It was degrading, so I wet myself a lot. The feeling of being drunk was different after having a head injury. The slowness about me that came—I guess from being dead for, well, who knows how long?—kind of made me feel drunk all the time. I was certainly now handicapped.

My family was so supportive in the hospital and after I got home. My stepdad installed bars in the shower so I could hold on to stand up. For the first six months after I got home, one of my sisters would have to help wash my hair and body every day while I held myself up with both hands. My sisters have always been my best friends. I owe them all so much.

About five months after I got home on November 7, 1987, my girlfriend, Barbie, gave birth to our daughter, Teddy. I was still very much confined to the wheelchair, but I was there in the delivery room to watch the birth. Barbie had to have a C-section, and I will never forget the way Teddy opened those beautiful blue eyes the second the doctor lifted her out. I was a very proud father. Teddy Lynn was the prettiest baby that was ever born. I couldn't stand up and hold Teddy, but I could sit in my chair and rock her just fine.

On January 5, 1988, Alice Cooper came back to Salt Lake City on his "Raise Your Fist and Yell" tour. My big sister, Kimberly, my girlfriend, Barbie, and I went to the show. It was impossible for me to see the stage because the concert was done in the exhibition hall of the Salt Palace. It was a general admission concert all on the ground level, no way to get up high enough to see. In my wheelchair, I was only about four feet tall. When the concert ended a lady who apparently felt bad for me came over to me and handed me two backstage passes. I was so shocked and grateful, but of course, wheelchairs can't go backstage. So I gave my passes to Barbie and Kimberly and told them I'd be out front, smoking.

About forty-five minutes later, they came outside to me. Barbie, in her hand, had a semi-glossed picture of Alice Cooper on it, and in black ink, it said, "Your pal, Alice Cooper, 1988." Barbie then said, "We talked to Shep Gordon, Cooper's manager, and we told him your story about speaking your first words after your coma, listening to our song." She then told me, "Cooper's manager told Cooper the story, and he signed this picture for you and has invited you over to his hotel room!"

I felt so nervous as Barbie pushed me across the street to the hotel. Whatever would I say to the legend, Alice Cooper? Didn't really matter what I would say. There's no way he could understand me anyway. Kimberly, Barbie, and I waited for the elevator to come down so we could go up. When the elevator door opened, out walked Alice Cooper! He reached down and shook my hand and said, "Did you enjoy the show?"

I just smiled and nodded my head; I didn't really even speak while we were with him. Barbie and my sister Kimberly spoke for me. We were with him for about fifteen minutes before a car came to take him to the airport.

A couple days after I met Alice Cooper, I started attending Cottonwood High School. Vocational rehabilitation made it possible for me to attend a regular high school because I was eighteen years old now, and my class graduated already. I guess it's one of the perks that come with having a head injury. A big yellow school bus would come to my house at 7:15 every morning. My stepdad, Charles, would wheel me down our long, steep driveway to the road and on to the lift on the back of the bus. The bus driver would strap me and my chair down, then turn the lift on and raise me up and into the bus. I felt so humiliated every time it happened. I only went to school for a couple of months and then just stopped; regular high school just wasn't for me.

A year after the accident, my family let me see my mom's car that I had rolled. We all thought that seeing the car would help me remember the accident or maybe help me remember a part of that day. We were mistaken; no memories came. They had left the car exactly the way they found it. Beer cans empty and on the backseat and floor, one of the cans was bent in and on one side, and little holes poked in with black residue surrounding the holes, and a hole on the side for a carburetor. Don't know why I'd never bought a pipe; I guess the homemade ones worked just fine. The frame of the driver's side door was bent out about a foot. It was hard to imagine that all of me fit through that bent frame.

I was trying to live my life the way I used to live with a disabled body. The part of my brain that told my body how to move was gone or the cells were dead anyway. Whatever, I could not drink alcohol like I once could and I could not live the fast-paced dope peddling life that I was so accustomed to living. My main source of income came from my selling pot to my incarcerated friend. It was pretty easy. I would get a quarter pound of my usual weed for $200, clean all the sticks and seeds out, then I would compress an ounce in to a baggie wrapped in duct tape and put into an empty cigarette pack. I would drive my car through the parking lot of the military base across the freeway from the prison until I saw a friend of my friend picking up garbage from the parking lot, which paid him 25 cents an hour. I would drive by him and throw my pot-packed cigarette pack out the window. He would then pick it up as if it was garbage and put it in the bag. I suppose he then went in the building and asked to use the bathroom, where he pulled the duct taped ounce bag out of the cigarette pack and put in up his backside.

    I did this once a week. That's four ounces or a quarter pound a month. I would get a check mailed to me for $1,000 from the state prison every month. There was no cash on the inside. Inmates have books, and when an inmate wants to send money out from their books, it goes out in the form of a check. The check would say "To: Darren H. From: The Utah State Prison." It kind of made me feel warm and tingly inside.

    Anyway, that was $800 profit off a $200 quarter pound; that was a pretty good profit.

    Pitiful, incomprehensible, demoralization—those were the words I heard read out of the book that made me realize that these people here knew what was inside me. On the twenty-ninth of September, 1988, I went to a 12-step meeting. Trevor had flown back to Salt Lake City. He had been living at one of his parents' houses in Austin, Texas. He came back to check into a treatment center. The only time I could visit Trevor was at these 12-step meetings. My big sister, Kimberly, went with me. For me to be able to walk, I needed a cane in my right hand and my left arm around her shoulder. She also went because she was in love with Trevor. What happened at that meeting I attended changed the entire way I thought about everything in my world. I had no idea that people could enjoy life with no drinking! I realized that there were people who didn't drink for religious reasons, but their "high on life" rush was given them by God or something like that.

In this meeting, all the chairs were filled by regular people who weren't dressed like religious people, and they didn't talk about religious ideas or concepts. The steps and traditions were up on the wall. I saw the word *God* a couple times in the writings. The word *God* was only used once or twice in the readings that I heard, but he was just politely mentioned like on money. This wasn't a big God conspiracy like I thought it might be. All these people at the meeting were clean and sober on purpose. They claimed that being clean and sober got them high! This was the craziest thing I had ever heard. Not taking drugs to get high? Madness! I remembered the first 12-step meeting that I had attended with Trevor five years ago at that fellowship hall, and I remembered Blaine and the disease that we both suffered from.

I sat back and listened to people get up and introduce themselves as alcoholics or addicts and that they lived their lives "*one day at a time*" without altering their minds at all. Then near the end of the meeting, a man got up and shared. His name was Roy. He shared about how he was sure that Ozzy Osbourne had found the 12-steps of recovery when he wrote that song, "Demon Alcohol." That statement excited me so much. I figured if Ozzy was into the 12-steps, then I could get in as well.

I found that the statement Roy made about Ozzy kept me sober for twenty-four hours, but that was long enough because twenty-three hours later, I was back at the next meeting, getting my next fix. That was how I stayed sober for the first year of my sobriety. I would hit at least one meeting a day. I found that I could do my life *one day at a time*. I really believed in the God concept. The whole destiny idea made sense. Everything in my life, all the tragedies and miracles, had led me up to this day. Me being clean and sober made sense. I didn't have another drink or any drugs for three years, six months, and five days.

On the second day of my sobriety, Roy had me meet him at a club called the Alan-O. I had my sister drive me down there. We met, then went downstairs for some coffee. After talking for a while about my life, Roy asked me if I read very much. I told him about only going through the ninth grade in school and about going to Valley Alternative only to sell drugs. I confessed to only having seven high school credits.

Then once again, he asked me if I read very much. I responded with, "I read newspaper articles and sometimes short stories."

Roy got up and walked over to a bookshelf on the wall. He then grabbed a big hard-covered blue book and tossed it over to me. It slammed hard on the table in front of me, *bam!*

I said, "Damn, Roy, that's a *big book!*"

He smiled at me and said, "That it is, and it's also a guide that will teach you how to live the rest of your life, clean and sober and happy."

I chose my first higher power on day sixteen of my sobriety. Her name was Liz, and she was an old party friend of mine who just disappeared one day. I ran into her at a 12-step meeting of a sister fellowship in that same treatment center where Trevor was staying. A lot of people, including myself, attended recovery based 12-step meetings in a few different fellowships. Liz and I were so happy to see each other that we hugged for five minutes. Then after the meeting, I took her out for coffee and then back to my house—well, my mom's basement anyway. She didn't leave for ten months!

Liz and I had a lot of fun together. That night that I ran into her, she was celebrating eighteen months of sobriety. I didn't know it at the time, but I was helping Liz do some step work. The thirteenth step: *Convincing the newcomer that you are their higher power and they should worship you on a daily basis.*

I truly did my part of worshipping her every day. She was so beautiful, and I was absolutely in love with her. We attended lots of meetings all over town. Fellowship Hall, where I did my first meeting in 1983, was closing down and being moved about twenty blocks east.

When I was about eight months sober, I went to my first conference here in Salt Lake City. It was May of 1989. It was a huge conference called ICYPAA (International Conference of Young People in

Alcoholics Anonymous), and it happens somewhere different in the world every year, but it happened in my hometown in the first year of my sobriety. I always considered that to be a God thing. I can still hear the chants we would all say, "ICY, ICY, ICY, PA, PA, PA." It was so amazing to see those people from all around the world coming together in the unity of recovery. What a beautiful G.O.D. (Group of Drunks) here in my city.

Whenever I hear that chant, I see in my mind a lady named Jill S. She had just gotten out of Federal prison; she went down on a huge cocaine bust. Jill was an old friend of Liz's. So when Liz and I got in a fight and she went to her mom's house for the night, I went to Jill's. The sex was amazing but didn't last as long as I fantasized it would; did I mention how hot Jill was? Liz and I just wanted different things. She relapsed a couple months after we split up. She had hooked up with a good guy named Chris who had moved down South and I hope is doing well; he is back in the program now. I Facebooked Liz recently, and she says she's doing well but is not in recovery.

*****

Saturday night here in D-pod. We are still locked down for dinner. I guess Sara and I are done. I called her earlier, and she said something that pissed me off, so I hung up on her. I called her back an hour later, and she hung up on me. So like I said, I think we're done. I already miss her face. Well, I hope they have a good movie on tonight. Easter Sunday, and I'm behind bars; hope my family has a nice day.

My Sara won't get to be with her family either today; too much drama there to even get into. I hope my daughter, Teddy, and her brother, Jaxon, go to my mom's for Easter. I'm sure they will. They'll probably take their little sister, Justice, and Teddy's boyfriend, Dan. I hope they have a fun day. My mom will be up sometime tonight to see me. I hate doing this to her.

*****

On the twenty-ninth day of September 1989, I celebrated my one year of sobriety. This was a very special day for me. Not only had I gone 365 days without a drink or a drug of any kind, but also because when I celebrated my birthday at my home group meeting, I walked from my seat halfway back in the room all the way up to the podium in the front of the room by myself with just my cane! Nobody was under my left arm, just me, and I didn't fall. All my family and all the people in the fellowship who had watched me and had helped me walk for the past year all stood up and cheered for me. I had never been so high in my life as that moment.

When the secretary called for anybody celebrating one year of sobriety, my sponsor, Roy, stood up and introduced me—it was truly magical! Roy always put off doing step work. He told me that now in your sobriety, there are just five things you need to do each day for a better life. Roy would count on his fingers in a way that was telling me to remember. He would say, "One, don't drink. Two, don't shoot dope. Three, don't die. Four, go to a meeting. And five, call your sponsor."

*****

Life today at the jail was kind of crazy. This morning for breakfast, we had oatmeal and biscuits and gravy. Quite satisfying, so I laid back down, first wrapping a towel around my head to block the light from my eyes. I slept kind of hard for a couple of hours but then was woken by a cop named Huff who made an announcement over the intercom. He said, "If you want to be out of your cell this morning, stand by your cell door now. If you don't stand by your door, then you can't come out until after lunch."

Now on Monday, Wednesday, and Friday, that meant 2:00 p.m., so I jumped out of bed and stood by my door. My cell was right by the guard station. The short bald cop we called Huff & Stuff looked over at me and then started walking toward me and then said, "Don't stand by your door in your underwear. What if there's a female officer here?"

I mumbled, "Fuck you."

I guess my speech is a lot clearer in the morning time than it used to be. Officer Huff walked into my cell and pushed me back and down onto my bunk. I could tell that he was surprised on how easy I was to move and how off balance I was. He then looked over at the wheelchair by the wall. I could tell he was shocked and sorry but still said, "You will not be coming out today!"

I was stunned by what had just happened. I put my head in my hands and just sat there on my bed, not really knowing what to do. I sat there for four or five minutes. The cop came back; I could hear him outside my cell door. He was asking the cop in the booth to open cell 6. Nothing happened, so again he asked, "Open 6."

I then heard my cell door slide open, and he walked in. He looked at me and said, "Sorry about what happened."

I said, "No, I'm sorry, sir, when I wake up in the morning, I'm not really sure where I am. I say the strangest shit."

He kind of smiled and asked again if I was okay.

I assured him I was fine. He then told me I was fine to come out.

The morning was fine; we racked back in our cells after lunch and then out again at 2:00 p.m. At 3:00, we were racked back in and were told the jail was on lockdown. The lock down started at 3:00 p.m. It's now 6:00 p.m. Who knows if we'll get out before bedtime?

Darrell went to court today, and apparently his new celli ate three of his top Ramen noodles while he was gone. Now Darrell is a stocky but short Black man who kind of has a temper. I consider him a good friend of mine; we play a lot of spades together, never on the same team, but we're tight.

The cop went into their cell and escorted Darrell's white roommate away. So I don't know if or when we'll ever get off lockdown. When we do, I will offer Darrell one of my noodles. I hate for people to be hungry, especially in here.

*****

I had made an agreement with my sponsor, Roy, and one with myself. With Roy, I told him I would go back to school. I told him that after I was one year sober, I would go to the community college and take a placement test. The agreement I made with myself was as soon as I had celebrated my first year clean and sober, I would start doing 12-step work in the county jail and the state prison. I felt a lot of guilt for all the dope that I had supplied to the prison, not only before I got sober, but I actually kept taking it out to the prison until I was ninety days clean and sober. I was very addicted to the money. That's when I officially asked Roy to sponsor me. I just felt like such a hypocrite making money selling drugs to the prison. I never did tell my sponsor about my moneymaking scheme at the prison, but I knew I had to make my amends to the prison, and running meetings out there on my free time would be my way to do it.

Becoming a volunteer at the prison and at the metro county jail was pretty easy. I got with Francis. He always introduced himself as "Francis the Great Big Alcoholic." He had me fill out some paperwork and then attend a seminar where they did a background check, and then I was cleared. I did two meetings a week in the state prison and two in the county jail. *"Half measures availed me nothing."* I started doing what is known as the two-step, step 1 and step 12—admit there's a problem and then go try to fix everyone else.

Taking the placement test at the community college was very time-consuming. I had to first make an appointment with Vocational Rehabilitation and then schedule a time to meet with an education counselor at the college; it took me about a month to finally take the placement test. Having had only one year of education in high school, I placed right near the bottom. Thank God that all you need to attend community college is someone to pay for it.

Vocational Rehabilitation certainly had my back, and they told me that they would cover tuition and the cost of books because of my traumatic brain injury (TBI). They said they would also cover me because I was an alcoholic or if I was an ex-convict. I certainly had two of the three qualifiers.

I started the winter quarter in January 1990 at the Salt Lake Community College (SLCC). My nickname back then was Prerequisite because I had to take all the lower education classes first before they'd let me take the higher education classes that I needed for my degree. Any class under a 101 doesn't count as college credit.

DARREN H.

I went twelve hours a quarter for twelve quarters and only earned eighty-three college credits. I really did enjoy learning; it was a bit frustrating trying to remember things with my TBI. A lot of the classes I had to take two or three times just to get a passing grade. The process for me to remember things with my having no short-term memory was about reading, writing, and hearing things so many times, just to get them to stay in my head.

After about four or five quarters in school, I met Callie. Callie was in a fellowship that dealt with people who were addicted to people like me, a fellowship called Al-Anon. We hit it off real well. We were both in love with my favorite topic: me. Eventually, we started attending the church of religious science, and before I knew it, we were married. It was very odd how unhappy I was. I mean, I must have known what I was doing, right? Callie was very beautiful and very blonde; the sex was great. She had a good job, made great money, and she was crazy about me.

I think the problem was that my ego was in control of me. I worked the graveyard shift in a gas station while I went to school in the morning, so I slept in the afternoon. I made only a little bit of money. Callie worked for an engineering firm where she made a lot of money. I guess my ego just couldn't cope. I guess I was just a moron. Anyway, I started looking elsewhere for different ladies to help me with my deflated ego. We had the marriage annulled after four months.

Double Down Doug became my sponsor after Roy relapsed, which happened in March of 1990 on my eighteenth month sobriety birthday. After Callie and I decided to call it quits, I moved in with Double Down for a while. I was still attending the community college. It was the summer of 1991. Danny, his nickname was Bubba. Bubba was my best friend. He called me Holmes. He and I were sitting outside the technology building, smoking. Bubba and I became friends just after I got sober. His sobriety was in April of 1988 and mine in September. He always kept the same sobriety date.

While we were sitting there, waiting to go to our next class, she appeared. I didn't even see her walk up; she was just all of a sudden sitting there, a little bit magical. I said hello to her, and she didn't respond. It took about three days of me saying hello before she responded back to me. All she said for the longest time was, "Hi." It became my favorite pastime sitting outside the technology building, waiting to say hello to her.

I waited her shyness out. Her name was Michelle, and I found myself loving someone more than I had ever loved before. At our beginning, she was very curious about the way that Bubba and I hugged whenever we left each other. Thinking back on it now, it does seem kind of strange, but we were such a big part of the 12-step program that it always felt proper. Anyway, Michelle shortly caught on, and soon she was *trudging the road of happy destiny* along with us. She became my girlfriend, and I gave her the nickname "Joplin" because her favorite rock star was Janis Joplin. Joplin and I were so perfect for each other. She was so sexy, and I had never been with anyone who made me feel the way she did. I felt so important. She could make my whole day perfect with just a smile. I think her love for me came from my waiting for her to become willing to get to know me.

She didn't really have a life; she had no friends at all. Joplin had been in a very bad relationship that had left her afraid of everything, but that soon changed. It took about three or four months, but she finally came out of her shell. She became very close to Snucums or Josie, Bubba's wife. She asked Snucums to sponsor her; Joplin had a pretty intense drinking problem.

By the end of the summer, we all attended an Alice Cooper concert together. It was the "Hey Stoopid" tour. Before the concert, Cooper gave an interview at one of the local radio stations. Bubba, Luther, T-Bone, and I went to the radio station to try and get a glimpse of the rock star. We got there about fifteen minutes before the interview, thinking that would be plenty of time to get a proper place to stand. We were sadly mistaken. There must have been seventy Alice Cooper fans crowded around the front door of that radio station when we arrived. We were forced to stand in the back of the crowd, closer to the back of the building.

When the interview ended, I guess to avoid the crowd, Cooper and some other guy came walking out the back door of that station.

It was so amazing because Cooper walked right over to me and said, "Hey, man, where's the chair?"

I had been out of the chair and walking with a cane for almost three years at that time. It felt so rewarding to be remembered by the great Alice Cooper. My pride and my ego grew so much and so fast that my head must have grown four feet in diameter. The problem with that was that my tongue also grew in diameter, so when I tried to respond to him, all that came out was, "Blah, blah, blah."

He gave me a big smile, tapped me on the shoulder, and jumped in the passenger side of a car. The other guy got in, and they drove off. The concert that night was, of course, amazing.

In January of 1992, I went to Wendover, Nevada, for my first gambling experience. I went with a man named Madesto. He was a patient with me in my third hospital after my car accident. He had a stroke. A stroke causes there to be a shortage of oxygen to the brain, so it is a brain injury. We stayed in touch on the telephone every now and then, but he had asked me if I would drive him just over the Nevada border to Wendover. He then offered to supply me with some money to play the dollar slots with him. I had never played a slot machine before, and Joplin was doing something with her mom, so I agreed to drive him out.

He and I spent a few hours playing dollar slots. I took $50 of my own money with me. When we came back home, I had $100 in my pocket. *That was pretty cool*, I thought. The next day, I asked my friend T-Bone if he'd like to drive back out to Wendover with me. He agreed to go with me, so out we went. I was playing a dollar slot called "Wild Cherry." I had one credit left on it. I hit the spin reels button, grabbed my bucket of dollar coins, and started to walk away.

All of a sudden, the Wild Cherry slot machine started making this wonderful sound with the bells and whistles. I stopped and turned around what I saw in the middle of the screen was "Wild Cherry, Wild Cherry, Wild Cherry." The rush that came over my head was like the first time I shot cocaine, but I was now three years clean and sober—what a rush! I had definitely found my new high; the $1 bet paid me $2,500.

I drove to Wendover every day after class on Monday through Thursday; it only took me about four months to give them back their money. My last time out, I lost a lot more than my money. Joplin and I got a ride out from a program friend that did maintenance at the community college. We all went out on Thursday afternoon. I remember it being odd because I usually just drove myself, and Joplin went with me a lot of the time, and I only took $50 with me each trip. It got to be about 9:30, and our friend that brought us out was ready to go home. I was playing a "7 Heaven" quarter slot machine and I was up about $500. When the pit boss saw me getting ready to leave, he came over and offered me a room for the entire weekend.

Joplin said, "I've got a feeling about this machine. We can't leave."

I agreed with her, so we stayed. I only remember going to the room once in those three days to fool around a little and for a couple hours of sleep, then it was right back to the casino floor.

Sunday morning came, and I was down to my last $50, the amount I had when I got there. We spent that real quick and then left the casino. I was so glum. I felt like I had lost so much because that quarter slot paid me so much, and I put it all back in. We walked up to the onramp for the I-80 freeway and stuck out our thumbs.

I love hitchhiking with beautiful ladies. The first vehicle by stopped. Some guy driving a little truck, he was a longhaired stoner dude. We knew about the stoner part because he immediately offered us a loaded pipe. I quickly responded to his offer by telling him about my car accident and that I was three and a half years clean and sober.

His response was, "I'm sorry," then he handed me the pipe back. I don't know why I felt justified in hitting off that pipe; I forgot that I'd be burning up a lot more than the pot in the bowl. Not only did I lose my three and a half years of sobriety but also the respect of Janis Joplin, and most important, the respect I had for myself.

Joplin stuck around for a few weeks, but then she was gone. Shortly after my relapse, my sponsor, Double Down, took off to sail around the world, so I had to move. I moved into a studio apartment and fell head over heels for a little cute redhead named Ann.

Ann liked to smoke pot and, well, I think that was all she really liked; the sex was all my liking. Ann turned out to be a lesbian; hope she's happy. I never did anything besides smoke pot until that fall when a friend of mine from my past put a gun in his mouth and blew the back of his head out. I got back with the old friends—or customers, you might say—from Valley High School to bury Brian. I was at a remorse party at Wendy's trailer. I drank a toast to Brian. I remember the way the whiskey burned my throat as it went down, very painful. The cocaine I snorted ten minutes after certainly killed the pain of the alcohol.

I waited about sixteen or seventeen hours before I put a needle back in my arm. Having no coordination meant that someone else had to shoot me up. My new best friend was actually an old customer. His name was Dan, and he was probably the biggest pot dealer in the Sandy area, in the mid-eighties anyway. Everybody knew Dan; his pager went off every couple minutes, twenty-four hours a day. Dan and I went to Brian's funeral together, and then afterward, we went to my apartment and shot cocaine for three days. I was quickly reminded about why cocaine ruled my life for those years before the accident. She tasted so good and was so addicting. I remember that time so well because that was the last time I shot coke. Dan showed me a way to break away from that death grip that cocaine had on me; it was called crank or better known these days as crystal meth.

I would shoot a quarter gram of coke and be high for like ten or fifteen minutes, then I'd start looking for shit to pawn to get more. I shot my first quarter gram of crank, and I was high for three days! The taste in the back of my throat certainly wasn't as good as the coke, and the high was different, but economically, it made sense. So I officially became a Crankster. I started selling pot again also; I needed money to get my new habit up and going.

I soon met Amanda through Bob. Bob was the guy who first shot me up, back when I was fifteen years old. Bob tried to keep Amanda a secret for so long because she was so beautiful, but the time came when his need for money overcame his need to keep her a secret. Amanda needed lots of pot to ship up to Oregon, and she needed to trade with this good go-fast or crank that she had. Bob knew that I was the right person to take care of this business. We peddled our dope back and forth for a few months. She just loved the dry lime green buds that I always had, and I loved the P2P-based crank they still made in Portland. Amanda would drive my buds up to Portland every couple weeks and return with the good go-fast.

I was always very attracted to Amanda, but my slowness in the way I walked and the way that I talked made me a lot less of a person in her eyes, and that's just how that was. Bob kept her a secret from me, and I was keeping her a secret from Dan. Dan was the one who everybody knew, and to make this distribution project take off, I knew that I would have to introduce these two. Dan and Amanda hit it off real well, like I knew they would. We all made a lot of money moving the crank and the pot.

In early 1994, Amanda and her kids moved back up to Portland, and they took Dan with them. I had just been thrown out of my apartment for having too much traffic or not paying rent or something like that. I moved in to the Volunteers of America (VOA) detox center where I lived for a month, waiting for a bed to open up in a treatment center called "the Haven." I didn't really want to get into treatment, but I had nowhere else to go. All my other bridges had been burned.

Finally, in the middle of February a bed opened up at the Haven, and I was able to move in. It wasn't at all what I'd expected, and the other residents didn't like me much, so they voted me out on my fourteenth day there. I then moved in to my mom and stepdad's for about a week, but all I could think about was going north to Portland to be with Dan and Amanda and all that good go-fast.

My mother could do nothing but cry the morning I left. My stepdad, Charles, drove me to the airport. He explained to me on the way that my mom didn't expect to see me alive again. I tried to convince him to assure her that I would be just fine.

I was excited to fly to Portland and see Amanda and, I thought Dan, but when I arrived, I found out that Dan had flown to Salt Lake earlier that same day. Amanda was about ninety minutes late picking me up from the airport. Amanda had changed, and I'm not really sure what it was, but we could not get along. After only about a week, she threw me out. I had brought four duffel bags with me to Portland. Walking with a cane meant I could only carry two bags at a time, so when I left Amanda's, I took two bags and walked about forty feet, then set them down, and went back for the other two. I did this for about an hour before I saw a gas station with a pay phone. I knew nobody else in the entire state of Oregon, so I called the only name I recognized in the phone book—Alcoholics Anonymous.

Two guys arrived about twenty minutes later and took me to some sort of a fellowship hall or a sober club. I sat around this club for about fifteen hours coming down off the meth that Amanda had shared with me. Finally, I fell asleep at one of the tables in the back, so they asked me to leave but first passed on to me some information. They told me of a place called "Northwest Passage Project." They said this place helped four people a day that were on SSI, but they only helped the first four in line, so I had to get there about 7:30 a.m. because they opened at 8:00. They gave me the address to this place, then called me a cab, and said goodbye.

The taxi brought me to a nearby motel where I got a room for the night. I got up at 5:00 a.m. the next morning and took a cab to that address. There were already three people in line when I got there. It was good that I took the advice to show up early. I met a man named James who told me how lucky I was to have been one of the first four in line, then he apologized for the budget and only being able to help a few a day. He gave me some vouchers for McDonald's and then told me of a hotel that they would put me up in. It was called the "Jack London," and it was located just a few blocks away from where we were.

For the next two months my address was 415 SW Alder, room 203, at the Jack London Hotel. It was a very old hotel. The door for the elevator was a gate that I would have to open and close by hand. A very nice crowd of people lived at the hotel—a bunch of junkies, whores, and thieves! I got my leather jacket stolen there. She was my first leather. On Christmas of 1988, I was eighty-eight days clean and sober, so my mom bought me a leather jacket. I had always wanted one but would always lose my jackets at parties or drunken endeavors, so Mom never would buy me one. When I got sober for real and stayed that way, she knew I'd take care of it. I walked out of my room at the Jack London for only a minute and was talking to my neighbor. Somebody walked into my room with an open door and walked out with my precious leather jacket. I was so sad for months.

After I had been at the hotel for a couple weeks, I met a man named Ralph. Everybody called him Red. He had red hair and a great big full red beard. Red had done a seven-year stretch up in the state penitentiary in Walawala, Washington, got out for a few months, then went back and did eight more years. So he had been down for fifteen years and had grown some pretty bad character defects. Our biggest difference was that I liked the way ladies' legs looked in pantyhose, and Red liked the way his legs looked in pantyhose. Our common interest was shooting and selling the crank.

Red had been shooting up for so long that he had "faded arm roots," which is to say that he had to administer his shoots in his neck. Red and I got an apartment together out on about 180th NE Glison, just outside of Portland. We met Tom through Tracy—or maybe it was Tracy through Tom, don't really remember. Tracy was the redhead who now owned my heart, and Tom-Cat was my new crank dealer who now owned my soul. I loved them both very much. Never did I have sex with Tracy, but we sure did have a constant foreplay attitude about each other. I think we were just too close of friends to screw things up with sex. She certainly helped me move a lot of go-fast all over Multnomah County.

Tom-Cat's affection for me was my pot connections in Salt Lake. All the pot in Portland and nearby Vancouver was so moist. Tom's crank connection loved the dry green buds that I would bring up from Utah. He was also very interested with the fact that there were six states in the country where the drug ephedrine could be bought over the counter, Utah being one of those six. Tom told me the famous P2P chemical used as the base for making the crank had not been being made for twenty years now, and their supply was running low. He then told me that ephedrine could be used as a base as well. I was then asked to fly down and get 50,000 ephedrine pills. I explained that I could only buy twenty at a time at the 7-Eleven, so 50,000 was just too many. I would fly down with a quarter-pound of the good go-fast taped to my legs and then back up with the lime-green buds. This seemed to make everybody happy. I was taken care of very well by my new friends in Portland and the old friends in Utah until I got busted.

I had gotten in a fight with Red. This did happen a lot. I didn't drink at all anymore; Red drank a half gallon of Rothschild Vodka every day. Every morning after he awoke, he would walk a mile to the liquor store and buy a half gallon, then come home and drink it. He was quite a violent drunk. The day finally came when I just couldn't deal with the yelling and the being pushed around.

One day, a neighbor called the cops because Red was screaming so loud. When they arrived, I asked if they could help me move up the street. They said they would take me. I moved in with Jamie and his mom, Sue. This is where my dealer, Tom, stayed as well. I don't think Tom was part of the family structure; he was just a friend of Jamie's. Jamie suffered from bipolar disorder so bad. I'm not really sure if he ever really lived in the real world. He sure liked the crank that Tom fed him, though.

There were two houses on the property. They let me live in the garage on the right. Jamie and Sue lived in the house on the left. When Tom would sleep and have people over, they would stay in the house where I was in the garage. I would pay Sue $400 a month, which was the same amount that I paid for rent with Red.

A couple weeks after I moved away from Red, someone gave him a shot in the neck, and they apparently missed. There was talk sometime after this about who gave Red the shot and that they missed on purpose. I didn't know anything about that. What I do know is that the next morning, Red took the train to the hospital to get checked out. He collapsed by the front door of the hospital and went into a coma. I went to the hospital on the third day of his coma. The nurse in the ICU called me because there were no living relatives, and my name was on the lease along with Red's.

When I walked into Red's room and saw what an abscessed head looked like, I was shocked. His head must have been a foot wide, and the skin covering his face was all so droopy. He did not look like a human person. Red died that night.

It was November 1994. Red had been dead a few weeks. Jamie had a bunch of traffic over to the house. I was in the kitchen at the house where I lived. All of my belongings were locked in the garage except for my butt bag, which was around my waist. I answered the door because Tom and Jamie didn't. It was the police. Apparently, Ken, a man I didn't know, perhaps seen a time or two in passing, was Jamie's father and owned the property. Ken apparently called the police, trying to get Tom-Cat arrested. The cops came in and search Jamie's room. What or who they found wasn't Tom or Jamie. They had fled out the window. Instead, they found Mia and Justin. They were both searched and they were clean. I was so grateful my pot and go-fast was locked in the garage.

Then the cop pointed to me and said, "Put your hands against the wall!" He searched me, and in my butt bag, he found my little plastic scale. I had no drugs on me, but the residue in the bowl of the scale was enough to charge me with possession. I was taken to the Gresham jail and charge with a third-degree felony PCS (Possession of a Controlled Substance). The jail was very crowded, so they let me go after I was booked.

I was done with Portland or perhaps Portland was done with me. Living with Jamie and Sue in the garage in the house on the right was over. I packed all my clothes and flew back to Salt Lake where an old friend of mine, Clyde, had a spare room for rent. I lived with Clyde for a few months, then moved in with an old friend named Charles for a few, then met this chick named Deanna that I knew but could not for the life of me remember where from. Through our discussion, we discovered that my last name and her maiden name were the same. She asked me if many years ago I told a "Big Mac" joke at a family reunion. I told her I had, and we laughed and laughed; then we did some crank together. I had found my new partner in crime.

Deanna was my dad's cousin, and we stayed in her dad's basement and we sold lots of the go-fast. One day, she told me that her friend needed some crank, and she needed an amount so large that we couldn't refuse. We had to drive it down south; she lived in a town called Fisher, Utah. When we got down there, we found that this lady's boyfriend had pounds of skunk bud. I loved skunk bud. We stayed for three days, and then all my crank was gone, so we decided to drive back up. Having no more go-fast and smoking so much pot, I was so tired and I fell asleep in the truck.

Deanna stopped at a grocery store in Cedar City for some water. Now Deanna liked to wear old hippie beads around her neck. She had long black hair, and she had a very assertive attitude. She was approached by two Iron County cops in the parking lot of that grocery store. I think they were just messing with her because of the way she dressed and looked. When they approached the truck, I was sleeping, but they woke me up and asked me for my identification. I gave them my driver's license, and they walked over to their car. I thought everything was fine; I had never been arrested in the State of Utah as an adult before. When the cops came back to Deanna's truck, they placed me under arrest. They told me I had an NCIC warrant out of Multnomah County, Oregon, for "fleeing from justice." I guess that's what they call it when you miss court. The Iron County police now had the right to search me, and search me they did.

*****

Each day when the afternoon medication cart comes through, I'm given one Neurontin (for nerve pain) to swallow right then in front of the nurse and one to keep to take before bed. Neurontin, or these days they have a generic pill called Gabapentin, are nice to have when a heroin addict friend rolls in and can't stop their legs from shaking. It feels good to be able to help ease someone's suffering. This day, I did not give it away. I just put it in my shirt pocket and forgot to eat it before bed. We were on lockdown for the rest of the day because of some fight in another part of the jail. The next day, the entire jail was searched. I think they do that just to remind us of who we are. My roomy and I were taken out of our cell and searched. I was asked what was in my pocket and told to empty it.

I said, "Two papers—one has a phone number and the other is a calendar." I then told him that my Chapstick was also in my pocket. I then put my hand in my pocket and removed the items.

The cop then ran his hand down the pocket on my chest and said, "What's that?"

I put my fingers on the spot where he stopped and felt the bottom of the pocket. Pushed down in the crease was that Neurontin I was given the afternoon before. I told the cop that it was okay, I was given the pill by medical the day before, I had just forgotten about it.

Last night, about 7:00, the cop on duty came to my cell and said, "Darren, you're on full restriction lockdown for seven days." So today is day one, and I'm not going to let myself get worked up by the bullshit politics that go down here in the jail. Getting locked down for a week for forgetting to take a pill that has no effect on me anyway, I think maybe God is telling me to write more and play spades less. Oh, that reminds me, yesterday morning in my commissary, I bought a pinochle deck of cards so I can relearn how to play. I learned pinochle when I was nine years old in Kansas City. My mom had a friend named AK that taught me how to play, but I'd forgotten.

The worst part about being locked down for a week was not being able to attend the weekly AA meeting that Terry brought in, and I had started a meeting with four other jailbirds that we did every day. I was back to praying twice a day. I'd forgotten how at peace working on my *Conscience Contact with my Higher Power* made me.

*****

The cops in Cedar City took me out of the truck, cuffed me, and then searched me. They found a quarter ounce of skunk bud in one pocket and an empty rinse bag in the other. Now a rinse bag is a bag that once had crank in it, so there's a little bit on the sides of the bag. I was waiting until I got home to have a little shot. Well, apparently my rinse bag had enough residue on it to charge me with another PCS (Possession of a Controlled Substance), a third-degree felony. So both Deanna and I were arrested and taken to the Iron County jail.

It was my first time in a jail in Utah, and it was very coincidental that the cell that became my new home for the next five days. It was was cell #123 because 123 was my code on all my dealers' pagers. I knew God was just playing with me. Deanna's dad bailed her out the next day, but it took her five days to raise the $500 to bail me out. I was so grateful to be able to bail out when I had a warrant in another state. Apparently, Portland didn't want to spend the money to extradite me on a little possession charge. So Justin, a friend of Deanna's, drove her down to bail me out.

I had been out of the Iron County jail for just four days. We were in Deanna's dad's basement when she told me that her friend, Joe, wanted to buy an ounce of crank, and he was willing to pay $1,000 for it. I said, "Cool, give me thirty minutes."

I called Charles and asked him to bring one over; he was there in about twenty minutes. This Joe guy came by ten minutes later. When Joe was leaving, he said, "I'll need another ounce tonight about 10:00." Then he asked me to meet him at the bar called the Dream on Club. Charles came back about fifteen minutes later to get his $700, and I told him that I'd need another one tonight. Charles left me another ounce, and I gave him the $300 profit that I had just made and told him I'd give him the remaining $400 in a couple days because Deanna and I were going to Wendover, Nevada, to gamble after our 10:00 stop at the Dream on Club.

We were lightly packed for our trip. We may not even get a room. Deanna liked to gamble like I did; why get a room if you're not going to get off the casino floor, right? But first to the bar. The Dream on Club was a topless dancer bar, so Deanna dropped me off and went to the gas station to fill the tank. I went in and sat at the bar by Joe. We watched the dancers for a few minutes. Joe then said, "Hold on a minute, I need to make a call."

I nodded my head, so he got up and walked to the pay phone. *Kind of strange,* I thought. I figured he was just calling the true owner of the money. That seemed to be the way that most drug deals went. Joe then walked back over to me at the bar and said, "Okay, bro, we're good. Let's go out to my car and do this." I got up and followed Joe to his car, he jumped in the driver's seat, and I in the backseat. I pulled the ounce out of my pocket and handed it to him. He handed me a thick stack of twenties. He then said, "I'm going back in the bar."

There appeared to be fifty twenties, there so I said, "Cool," and started counting the money.

When I got up to about $400 dollars, suddenly a loud voice yelling through a bullhorn said, "Don't move, and put your hands in the air!"

Six members of the DEA (Drug Enforcement Agency) were standing at the front of the car. All six had their guns pointed at me, and in my hand was a $1,000 of their money, no doubt. One of them walked to the back door of the car and opened it. He then smacked me in the face, knocking my glasses off, and then sprayed both of my eyes with the pepper mace. It burned so bad, unless my eyes were closed; I guess that was the purpose of the mace. I was pulled out of the car and brought down abruptly onto his knee. My rib was broken and I couldn't breathe, but all I could think about was how bad my eyes hurt. I then heard Deanna's voice; but how could that be? The medics then douched my eyes out.

Dan was the top dog of the DEA unit, and he told me that if I wanted to talk with Deanna and ride to the jail with her, then I would have to let the doctor at the jail wrap my rib. If I wanted to go to the hospital in the ambulance, then I would not even be allowed to talk with Deanna. I told him, "Okay, you win, I'll just let the jail wrap me." I've busted ribs before, and I knew there was nothing special at the hospital.

On the ride over, Deanna told me that when she returned from the gas station and saw all the cop cars and then the ambulance, she turned herself in and said we were together out of concern for me, my sweet cousin. Not too sure if I'd have done the same thing. To jail together again we went; this time it was Salt Lake County Metro Jail on 400 S. and 300 E. This time was a second-degree felony, distribution charge.

I did fourteen days in jail before pretrial let me out. The judge told me that they had to hold me because Multnomah County in Oregon had fourteen days to decide if they wanted to pay to have me extradited. I guess they didn't. Deanna just did three days until she bailed out, thank God.

I went to my first court date about a week after I got out. My public defender told me that the prosecution would drop my charge from a second to a third-degree felony if I waived my preliminary hearing so the rat didn't have to testify in open court. When the DEA approached the car, I had $1,000 of their money in my hand. I had no way that I could beat these charges. A second-degree felony has a one to fifteen year prison sentence that goes along with it, where a third-degree felony only has a 0 to 5 year sentence attached to it. So I figured that's ten years; I might as well take the deal. In waiving the preliminary hearing, I was admitting guilt, but my public defender told me that he'd keep getting sentencing put off for as long as possible, which was good with me.

It was the middle of June 1995. Deanna and I were living in a hotel in downtown Salt Lake on South Temple called the Carlton. The police came to our room looking for somebody else. Once they saw that they weren't there, they left. An hour later, the same cops showed back up and said, "Darren H, Portland wants you now!" So back to Salt Lake County I went for another fourteen days, waiting for Portland to have me shipped on up there.

On day number fourteen, the guard yelled, "Darren, roll up!" I was so relieved that Portland still didn't come for me. As I was grabbing my clothes and toiletries, I was passing out all my candy bars and other commissary to my bros in the cell block. I was taken downstairs put in the room to take off my orange jumpsuit and put my street clothes on, and then out to where they release you from. I could see the 7-Eleven across the street and could almost taste that first cigarette. All of a sudden, a big burley ass cop grabbed me by my back-belt loop and pulled me into the garage. I was then driven from the Salt Lake Metro jail to a jail in Burley, Idaho, where I had lunch. I was then put into a different car and driven to Ada County jail in Boise, Idaho.

The next morning, I was put into a van with two other guys. We drove from Boise, Idaho, to Pendleton, Oregon, where we stopped at a jail and picked up three more guys. Then we drove to downtown Portland to the MCDC (Multnomah County Detention

Center) where I lived for three days on twenty-three hours a day on lockdown. Then I was moved to a jail about one hundred blocks east called Inverness for two days. Next, they moved me to a jail called the Farm; it was in Gresham. They considered me too handicapped to live at the Farm, so back to Inverness I went.

When we got back to Inverness, they walked a group of about twenty of us down a long hallway. We would stop at each of the sections and drop one or two guys off. I was getting mad because I thought with my disability, I should have been housed in one of the first sections; but no, they made me and one other guy walk all the way to the last section, #9. They opened the door, and in we went. As soon as I put my stuff on my bunk, I turned around, and there was Tom-Cat. My God has a sense of humor, that's for sure.

The only guy in the whole state of Oregon that I would consider my friend was Tom. We talked for a couple hours about our arrests and about Sue and Jamie. It was sure nice to see a familiar face. Then I heard those magical words, "Darren, roll up!" I had no idea what they could be doing now or where I was going. After I rolled my bedding up, I walked with a guard to the front of the jail to change my clothes and get my property. The lady at the cage told me that my father had bailed me out and she had the money from him to take a taxi to the airport where there was a ticket waiting for me. I was very surprised that my dad did all this for me, but I was very happy and on my way back to Salt Lake City.

When I arrived at the Salt Lake International Airport, my big sister, Kimberly, was waiting to give me a ride. She took me to Deanna's where there was a big fat shot of go-fast waiting for me. We shot crank for three days, and then slept for twelve hours. Deanna and I talked about our business and about the probability that I may have to serve some time. I had three third-degree felonies in three different counties in two different states. Now the one up in Portland, my first, I was put on probation and was transferred to Salt Lake, but I still had to be sentenced on the one in Iron County and Salt Lake County, Utah. Sobriety sure seemed like the easier softer way. It was now the seventeenth day of July 1995.

July 18, 1995, was my clean and sober date for fifteen years and is still the date of my last drink. Deanna and I got sober together; we went to our first 12-step meeting on the eighteenth. We did meetings like we did everything in our lives—to excess. *Half measures availed us nothing.* We hit at least two meetings a day. We celebrated our thirty-day, sixty-day, and ninety-day birthdays together. Our ninety-day clean and sober date was on the sixteenth of October, which was also my sentencing date for the attempt to distribute charge in Salt Lake, which was my second arrest in Utah; but for some reason, this sentencing date was first. We hit the noon meeting at the Alano club to celebrate our birthdays, and then we had to catch a ride immediately after to be downtown to the courthouse by 2:00.

My public defender told me that he wasn't sure what the judge was going to do. I was pretty sure I knew, so in preparation for this date, I had an operation that I always dreaded. Two weeks prior to this sentencing date, I had major surgery done on my left Achilles tendon. "Achilles lengthening" was the name of the operation; the reason for the operation was to allow me to stop walking on my tippy toes. I needed surgery done on both tendons ever since my coma, but each operation meant six more months in a wheelchair. I was so freaked out about getting back in a wheelchair after my two years of being confined to one.

My decision to have my first operation now was to get pity or some love from the judge. I rolled into the court room with Deanna pushing me. I had on a new leather jacket and my ninety chip in my hand when the judge sentenced me. Judge Atherton looked down on me from her throne and said, "Zero to five years in the state penitentiary." That was all she said. I was waiting for her to say something like "Suspended upon completion" of something; but no, that was all she said! A big plain-clothed cop walked up behind me and said, "Is there someone here that can take your coat?"

Deanna walked over as I removed my leather jacket. I hugged her and gave her my coat, and then Mr. Plain Clothes pushed me through the door to the jail part of the court.

I was in jail for three days before they drove me out to the prison. I prayed a lot in those three days. I didn't understand why

I was expected to do *ninth step* work in making amends to the state when I was only on my first step! I kind of gave my God a piece of my mind while I was in that little six-by-twelve cell, but I still knew that I was part of a bigger plan. I was a little scared; actually, I was scared to death. The morning came when they rolled five of us up and let us put our street clothes on, then put us in a van and drove us about fifteen miles south of the city to the state penitentiary.

R&O (Receiving and Orientation) is where we were taken; it was a section of the prison called Uinta 5. Getting checked in was just like being booked at the jail—a picture, fingerprints, housing assignment—well, in R&O anyway. This is where you wait for a bed to open in general population. Because of my being in a wheelchair, they told me they were afraid to house me with just anybody, so they put me in A-pod, otherwise known as the hole. What made the hole different from the other sections of R&O was a solid door about three feet outside the bar door. You could never see any of the other inmates except your cellie. We in R&O were on twenty-three hour a day lockdown. For one magical hour a day, each of the eight cells in A-pod got out. Each of the other seven solid doors was locked closed, so you couldn't interact with other inmates in the hole while you were out for your hour.

The thrill of that one hour a day was the shower. Praise God for the shower! Outside of the cells was a walking area; well, the hallway is what it was. It was seven feet wide by about fifty feet long with two solid doors on each end. The shower sits at one end of the hall; it's about three-by-six feet with a shower curtain and a white shower chair. The guards would bring in a large garbage bag for me to put my left leg in; I would tuck the top of the bag in to the top of my brace. After the shower, the rest of the hour was spent walking back and forth in that fifty-foot hallway. For me, being unable to put any weight at all on my left leg, I just cruised in that space in that prison-issued wheelchair. It was certainly nice to be out of that cell for an hour a day.

The biggest problem with living in the hole was the other inmates that went there when they were in trouble, and some of them would rebel. The thing that most happened was that they would blow the power out through a light socket in the cell. The lights would go out in the whole A-pod; this happened a lot. The guards were so tired of turning the power socket back on that they would leave us in the dark for days at a time. I guess the troublemakers thought that if they stirred up more shit, it would be better for them. It was quite miserable. I was truly *powerless and my life was unmanageable*. I guess God was helping me with my *first step*. I was in R&O for four weeks, and then a guard told me that next week, I would be transported down to the prison in Gunnison, Utah, for the night and then taken to Iron County for sentencing the next day. He then told me, "You would be best to write the judge a letter tomorrow and beg him to run that third-degree felony in Iron County concurrent with the one you're on now." I figured, what have I got to lose? So I did.

When I arrived in Cedar City, the judge thanked me for the letter. He told me he'd received it the day before. The judge told me, "Yes, I will run this charge concurrent with the one you're serving now." So instead of being consecutive—meaning do one, then the other—I got to do them concurrent, both at the same time. This meant I would not be down for more than five years. This was good news!

I smiled all the way back to Gunnison and then all the way back to Draper the next day. When I got back to R&O, I thanked that guard for suggesting I write the judge a letter. I did one more week in A-pod and then got moved to general population. They moved me to the old 288, which is now called Timpanogos. It was called 288 because there were four buildings which were called stars. Each of the stars had seventy-two cells. Because of the amount of people needing to be there, they had to put an extra bed in each cell. So instead of calling it 288 times two, they just decided on naming it after one of the mountain ranges here in Utah. Actually, all of the different sections in the prison are named after mountain ranges.

At Timpanogos, in between star two and three, was an office building for medical and visits, and in between star one and four was the chow hall. In the middle was a yard with a big cement walkway that was in a circle, and in the middle of the circle was grass. I had done volunteer work here at Timpanogos from 1990 till I relapsed in 1992; I ran the meetings in star four. I worked for a lady named Sylvia. I wondered if she still worked out here; oh, the irony.

I fished in to star two, A dorm. My first thirty days, I was on 9:00 lockdown, but after that, it was changed to 10:00. I quickly inherited the nickname "Wheels" which I must say is a lot better than "Tippy-Toes," which I'd probably been called without the operation. Cons kind of call it like they see it. I got my left sock, which is to say from my ankle to a couple inches below my knee, tattooed—skulls, demons, Vikings, cheese holes; you know, a prison tat. In the middle of the pair of skulls was a banner, and in this banner, it said "Wheels."

On one of my first days there, I rolled over to star four to see if Sylvia still worked here. She did and she remembered me. She was shocked to see me in a prison uniform. We talked for a while, and I proudly told her I was almost six months clean and sober again; she was pleased. On the east side of the chow hall, there were two metal pods. I asked Sylvia what those were used for. She told me that USU (Utah State University) had a distance education site here in those pods. I later found out that the classes happened on the USU campus up in Logan, Utah, but there was a television camera and a monitor and was broadcasted to eight or nine different locations; three of those locations were here at the prison, one here in Timpanogos, called "Bluff Dale North," one over in the Oquirrh 5 Annex called "Bluff Dale South," and one where the ladies were housed in Olympus called "Bluff Dale East."

A few days after I had learned about these wonderful educational chances for the inmates, I took a test to see if I was bright enough to take classes from a university. By the grace of God and a little bit of educational footwork I did at the community college a few years back, this ninth-grade dropout tested in to USU. For the next two years, I took every psychology and every sociology class they taught. It wasn't really that I loved to learn, and it was still very hard to remember things, but when I was in class, I wasn't in my cell, so it helped time fly by. The first ten months, I was at the "Bluff Dale North" site, then when I was moved to the other side of the prison,

I attended the "Bluff Dale South" site. The cost of school was always the same, no matter how many classes I took—$45 a quarter covered tuition and books, and I did have to return the books at the end of each quarter, but what the hell. The food in prison was very bad, it was always very noisy, there were no women anywhere, but school and tattoos were very cheap.

I had quite a bit of money while I was in prison. The State Government who locked me up never told the Federal Government who paid my Supplemental Security Income (SSI) that I was locked up. So my money kept coming to my house. I would have a friend grab my checks, cash them, and put the money on my books. It wasn't much, but all you could buy was $50 a week on commissary, and my little television cost me $9 a month to rent. This left a couple hundred dollars a month with nowhere to go, so I found a place for it. A bag of Bugler tobacco at the grocery cost about 99 cents, the same bag of Bugler tobacco in the penitentiary went for $100! I would send money from my books to a bro's wife. A couple days later, she would come and visit him.

The next day, during yard time, I would receive my hundred-dollar bag of Bugler. There were always little pocket-sized Bibles in all the stars in Timpanogos, and a page from the Bible torn in half was a perfect-sized rolling paper.

I saw the Board of Pardons after I was there ninety days. The board told me that because I was there on two nickels or two third-degree felonies running concurrently, I needed to be there for twenty-four months. Don, the board member I was talking with, told me that I could also write the treatment center, "Odyssey House," a letter, and if I could get a bed there, then they would let me parole there as soon as possible. So I immediately wrote and sent a letter to Odyssey House. It took ten months before I got a bed there. Once there, I only lasted fifty-three days, then they threw me out for not being willing to change, and back to prison I went. I couldn't deal with the form of treatment used on the Odyssey. They didn't use the 12-steps. Instead they used what's called "Gestalt therapy," where they break you down into dust and rebuild you like a Frankenstein!

When I got back to the prison in Draper, they put me on the other side, the Oquirrhs.

I left the prison in August of 1997, but I didn't leave Utah State University. I paroled to a treatment center called St. Mary's which was located in downtown Salt Lake. I transferred my studies to the Salt Lake Distant Education Campus, which was a lot more expensive than going to school in prison. Thank God Vocational Rehabilitation still had my back; they will cover you if you have a handicap, are an alcoholic, or if you're an ex-convict. I now qualified for all three categories. It took me eight months to graduate St. Mary's. In that time, I continued to attend USU and I also had my other tendon operated on. The bus ride to school and the two flights of stairs at my treatment center made the wheelchair a real experience, but I got through it.

Trying to be focused on my recovery and on my treatment, I would only take one or two classes each quarter; actually, the quarters had now changed over to semesters. When I graduated St. Mary's, I moved to transitional housing where I lived for two years. It was cheap enough that I could afford it on my SSI. I was saving for a car but didn't have one yet. So I would take the bus every day to school and to the Alano Club or Fellowship Hall for my meetings.

In April of 1998, just a couple weeks after I had left St. Mary's, I met Sheryl at a noon meeting at the Alano Club. She was a bit older than I, but I could tell in her eyes she had a GOD (Gift of Desperation) in her. I had almost three years of sobriety, and she was picking up her first thirty-day chip, so I knew we were perfect for each other. She had the right amount of innocence in her to be exciting to me. After the meeting, we hugged for a while, then I asked her for a ride home; that's how it all got started.

Sheryl and I were together for eight years. So much of my recovery I owe to that lady. We did so many meetings together. We both did 12-step work with the kids in the detention center. We both sponsored a handful of people. Our lives were about carrying the message, "*Half measures availed us nothing.*" In the year 2000, I got cleared by the prison to come out and do meetings again. They thought how my story was a full circle and that it would be good for the inmates to hear. Most people that relapse don't make it back.

I moved from my transitional housing apartment after my two-year lease was up; this was in the year 2000. Sheryl and I got an apartment together at a place called the Ritz; it was on South Temple and E Street, downtown Salt Lake. This is where we were living on September 11, 2001. Sheryl was at work, and she called and told me about the first plane. I then turned on the television and watched the second plane hit. Something changed inside me at that moment. I was so angry and sad at the same time. When Sheryl got home, we ran down to the craft store and bought a bunch of red, white, and blue beads and hundreds of safety pins. We then spent days making American flags to sell and send the money to the Red Cross in New York.

I was juggling my credits between USU (Utah State University), SLCC (Salt Lake Community College) and the U of U (University of Utah). At that time, I was taking a sociology class from a professor at SLCC, and she was from New York; thank God her family was safe. We lived there at the Ritz until the end of 2002. I remember the 2002 Olympic torch was run right up South Temple in front of the Ritz on its way to the university.

In early 2003, Sheryl and I moved from the Ritz to a house on 300 South and in between 6th and 7th East. We rented a house that sat three houses up from Jeannie and Clyde's house. Now these two people were the most spiritual people I knew. I met Clyde when I first got sober in 1988. Everybody called him *eleventh-step* Clyde because he always talked about the prayer and meditation. Sheryl and I actually moved there to be close to them, and we attended a study group at their house every Friday. The book we studied was called ACIM—*A Course in Miracles*. We loved that group so much that when Jeannie started to get sick, we moved the meeting up to our house.

In May of 2003, I received my associate's degree in general education from SLCC (Salt Lake Community College), and in September 2003, I received my bachelor's degree in interdisciplinary studies, emphasis in sociology and psychology, from USU (Utah State University).

I had a great desire to get a job using the degree that I had earned. I thought, finally, instead of volunteering to carry the message and help others, now I could get paid to do so. I was sadly mistaken, although I had many job interviews, and people pretended like they were impressed. I was always told that I hadn't enough education or that I just wasn't right, or my favorite line was, "You sound like you're drunk." So in 2004, I joined up with a program guy that used to attend ACIM named Tom. Tom had a business that went broke, and he wanted to use me—or my good name anyway—to be the president of a corporation. The business was about putting handicapped people to work selling products over the phone. My job entailed managing and distributing the money. I would also deliver most of the products sold by my telemarketers. Working with people who have physical handicaps turned out to be very rewarding.

After six months with the corporation, I was able to call SSI and tell them that I no longer needed them to send me money.

Clyde passed away in 2004, and shortly after that, we moved east up to Holladay, Utah, about 4600 South and 1300 East. We brought the ACIM meeting with us. It was just a little one-bedroom house, but it had a huge deck and a beautiful yard. We would have ACIM on the deck in the springtime; it was very serene. On Fridays, after the course ended, program friends of mine would come over and play poker. This became a very religious activity for many of us. It was fun; there was a twenty-dollar buy-in and there was a $2 limit on the bets; it was just fun times.

That weekly poker game lasted for about five years. In 2005, my daughter and her mother got into a fight. Teddy asked me if she and her boyfriend, Charles, could move in. Of course, I said yes, and it was wonderful having her there every day. I would cook them dinner every night, the four of us had a lot of laughs, and sometimes it was five of us because Teddy's friend, Ashley, stayed over a lot. We all had jobs and we all respected each other; it was a small house, but nobody ever seemed uncomfortable. Sheryl and I had our recovery, we both still sponsored a handful of people—and I even sponsored people in the state prison through the mail—and we kept hosting ACIM every Friday.

One day, my ego started working on me. I was about thirteen years clean and sober. Having this much sobriety was dangerous for my ego. I thought it felt so good to be called an old-timer, but the grandiosity and the smugness seemed to take me over. I believe my ego or my lower self was always working on me, but my higher self or my spirit was too busy to hear it. Something happened, and I'm not even sure what it was, but I started to dwell on the pain that I had in my legs, especially my knees. My ego thought I could take narcotic pain killers to deal with the pain. It told me that I could stay in recovery the same as I was and keep my serene piece of mind if I ate my narcotics as prescribed by my doctor.

Sheryl was the first to feel the change in me; I was truly rotten to her. I became a self-seeking pig-dog run riot. I was always such a free spirit because that was my choice. Once I started eating the narcotics, the switch in my head would no longer allow me to make my own choices. I was once again locked in a world where my ego made all decisions for me.

Sheryl didn't stick around for very much longer. I was no longer in love with her; I was only in love with me. She didn't move very far away, and we hit meetings together for a while then she moved up north. As time went on, my head kept telling me that the pain in my knees was getting worse and worse, so I would ask my doctor for more and more of the Tylenol-based painkillers like Lortab and Percocet.

I first met Sara on a Monday in late February 2008. I was at my home group meeting when Sara got up and read a portion of Chapter 5. She had the prettiest red hair and green eyes; she was the springtime. I approached her after the meeting and asked her how she spelled her name. She told me, "S-A-R-A;" I then lifted up my left hand and showed her that her name was tattooed on the top of my four fingers. I told her that Sara was my girlfriend when I was fourteen, so I stole a bottle of Indian ink from eighth-grade art class and tattooed it. I could tell she was surprised and delighted. I could tell right away that Sara was going to be a big part of my life.

*****

    Today was the twenty-ninth day of April 2014. I called my mother first thing this morning. She told me that Sara had spent all of my SSI money, then told me how dumb it was to let her come to the jail and get my debt card out of property. All I could do was agree with her. "Drug court" came into the jail this afternoon and interviewed me today. The interview was done by a very nice lady. By her accent, I could tell she was from the east coast. The interview, to me anyway, seemed to go well. She told me the decision on whether I could get into drug court or not was not up to her but up to the drug court attorney. I was then told that their attorney would contact my attorney. I told her about my court date on the fifth of May and asked her if their attorney will have contacted my attorney by then. She was unsure.

    When she interviewed me, she asked me questions for about thirty minutes. The first bunch of questions was about medical, questions about my head injury and my mental abilities and disabilities. The next questions were about my criminal history going back to my first arrest as an adult. She didn't care about my juvenile record, which was expunged after I got out of the hospital in 1987 anyway; next, we talked about my drug use. She said, "I'll name a drug, and you tell me when you first used it and when you last used it." She, of course, started with alcohol; everybody starts with alcohol.

    I told her, "I first tasted alcohol when I was eight years old, which was 1977, the same year I started smoking pot." I then told her, "My last drink was on the seventeenth of July 1995, and the last time I smoked pot was the thirteenth of September 2013, the day I checked in the hospital to come off the heroin."

    She then asked me when I started using heroin.

    I told her, "When I was sixteen years old, I started shooting water-soluble Dilaudid, which is synthetic heroin." I then told her about my dad's little brother, Uncle Danny, and how he was a heroin addict. I said to her, "Because of my uncle, I was so afraid of becoming a heroin addict that when I did the Dilaudid, I would never shoot them more than one day in a row. As far as shooting heroin goes, I probably only did it four of five times over the last twenty-eight years. Last year, starting in January, I went crazy and shot a gram of heroin every day for about nine months."

She then asked me about pain pills.

I said, "My introduction to pills was when I was a boy and was struck by a car." I then explained the story about the Soma in my life. I then told her, "my Doctor at the pain clinic gave me three-hundred Roxy's (Oxycodone), 30's every month." I then told her my last use was when I got into the heroin. I said, "I could shoot four Roxy's at a time or I could sell four Roxy's for $80 and then buy a $20 bag of heroin. Shooting the $20 bag or the two-tenths of a gram would kill the same pain as shooting the four Roxy's, but now I have $60 left over. Economically, it made sense." I then told her that this was the kind of stinking thinking that got me here.

Lastly, she asked about crystal meth. She planned on having cocaine being the question, but I answered both drugs together. I said, "I first shot crank just after Brian's funeral in 1992, and that was the last time that mean bitch cocaine had her vicious hands around my neck. And I first shot coke in 1984." I finished up by telling her, "The last time I shot go-fast was the day before I came here to this paradise."

She smiled and laughed a little. She told me that she had heard some good stuff from me and some bad. She wasn't sure what the "drug court's" attorney's decision would be. As we got up to leave the room, I asked her, "What shall I do now?"

As she looked out into the common area at the inmates walking in a big circle around the steel tables, she said, "Walk, I guess."

*****

Sara had accepted my request to go have coffee after we had talked for a while. She was truly like no other lady I had met before. Now you must understand that the women I usually pursue have generally been driven hard and put away wet; that was just kind of how I rolled. They needed a knight in shining armor to come and save them, which made me feel important. Sara had only been with one man her entire life. She married her high school sweetheart. She told me she had been married for fourteen years and had two children, and then she told me she was no longer happy. We hugged and kissed before she left, and it felt so right.

Emily #43023 was the only reason I couldn't fall in love with Sara. Emily was an inmate in the Utah State Prison that I had been writing to for six months. Now she eventually started calling as well. I had never had a relationship that wasn't built off a lustful desire. I never even knew what she looked like until she sent me a picture a few months after we started writing. She was very pretty. It was kind of weird how she looked just like her voice sounded.

Emily had gotten my name and address from a guy that I sponsored. She had my information for quite a while ever since she was working in the kitchen back in the county jail six months prior. One day, I just got a letter, so I read it and wrote her back, and it became an addiction.

Sara became homeless, which was kind of nice, and I don't mean that in a rude way. What I mean by nice was that she could stay all night when she came over. Her parents had asked her to move out; her husband and her kids could stay, but she had to go. Her husband, Brandon, told her that he hadn't loved her in ten years. Sara and her father did not get along. He had been dry off the booze for twenty years, but he had no program, which is to say he never worked on himself. He was certainly on a vicious dry drunk; he was so mean to Sara.

Sara, Brandon, and their two kids, Ryan and Sara, lived with Sara's parents since they had come back from Las Vegas. They were in Vegas because Brandon was in school, paid for by Sara's folks. Sara's job was as a stay-at-home mom, so where the home was didn't really matter, but living with her dad wasn't part of the job. She would rather sleep in her car in a parking lot than at her dad's house; so, of course, I let her stay at my house.

I got real used to having that sweet little red flower around, but Emily #43023 paroled on April 5. I didn't know what to do, so

I did nothing. I did drive up to Ogden, Utah, the day she paroled. I wanted to pick her up at the prison in Draper, but Emily's dad wanted that job. When I got up to Ogden and we saw each other for the first time, it was nice and we hugged for a while, and then went for a drive and talked. I all of a sudden was worried about Sara and if she was okay. I knew that I was wronging Sara just by being there at Emily's in Ogden. I was honest to her and told her what my intentions were, which were to see if I could be happy with Emily. But I kept sleeping with Sara after I told her about my intentions.

All of a sudden, up in Ogden, I felt so bad about how what I was doing must have made Sara feel like shit. I couldn't drive back from Ogden fast enough. That night, I finally got real with Sara. I now wanted her and just her, and she knew. My recovery was a bit tweaked because of the painkillers I took for my knees. Sara took stuff for pain as well; we never switched our painkillers in the beginning.

Sara had cancer in her throat; she did radiation therapy, which I understand is quite painful. She was on some sort of patches for the pain. Sara would fall asleep in our 12-step meetings all the time. I felt so bad for her; she tried to fit into my sober world. She only had a few months of sobriety, and she once had a big drinking problem, or so she said.

*****

Today is the thirtieth day of April, 2014, and I'm on my fourth day of lock-down. I got two letters in the mail today, one from my mom and one from my Sara. The one from Sara made me so happy, and the one from my mom so angry. Sara was able to spend some time with her kids. My mother was still unable to get my belongings from my house. Apparently, because of all the meth smoked in that house over the past twenty years, the walls were so saturated that the house had been condemned! Everything that I had in this whole world was in my master bedroom downstairs in that house. Things like my computer, VCR, DVD player, stereo, desk, my college degrees, television, camping gear, all my clothes—those were things that could be replaced. Things that couldn't be replaced were pictures my grandmother painted for me, all my photo albums, my autographed picture from Alice Cooper, the DVD that I burned of the news story about my car accident. I hoped she could retrieve my belongings soon.

*****

Problems with my job started happening in 2009. The customers my telemarketers had were all of a sudden broke. People didn't have enough money to take care of themselves, let alone help out the handicapped people. Each week, we continued to make less and less until finally we went out of business in 2010. Sometimes I feel like if I'd have had a clear mind, perhaps I could have saved the corporation, or my guilty ego likes to think so. I finally called SSI back and told them that I needed to start the process of getting my money back. I was attracted to the lovely voice on the phone, so I kept dishing out the compliments.

Now my voice—because of my partially paralyzed vocal cords—is very deep and slow and groggy, but I guess some ladies like that. Anyway, after about an hour on the phone and about four or five rude-ass glares from Sara, I got my monthly benefits back from SSI.

Sara's cancer was now in remission, but she was still in so much pain, or so she told her doctor anyway. My doctor told me that the acetaminophen level in the Percocet's that I was consuming was too high for my liver and that he was going to send me to the "pain clinic." My very first visit to the clinic, I was prescribed three-hundred Oxycodone 15mg, which have an opium base, not an acetaminophen base. The scribe read, "Take two pills five times a day as needed for pain."

My second visit to the pain clinic, the following month, I told the doctor my knees were still hurting too much. So he upped the 15s to 30s, and I received that amount on the fifth day of each month. I had just made a new best friend—he was my doctor feel-good!

When the corporation was going, I would bring home $500 a week, but now back on SSI meant I would only receive $700 a month. Sara didn't work, and all of a sudden, I didn't have a way to pay my bills. My rent alone was $700 a month, which was all right when Sheryl and I would split it. I was in trouble and I got scared. I needed a way to make money and stay on SSI so my Medicaid would stay in place for my medical costs. Selling Roxy's or Oxycodone was the only solution my altered mind could come up with.

Sara was her own person but never really in recovery, so she was quite easy to manipulate. I was prescribed ten 30s a day, and Sara was prescribed sixteen 30s per day. Apparently, we were both in quite a bit of pain. We never took all the pills we were prescribed. How could we? We had bills to pay. We sold our Roxy's for $20 bucks a piece, and in no time at all, we had too many customers to take care of.

Our attendance at our 12-step meetings slowed way down. I kept attending my home group meetings in each of the fellowships I belonged to for about a year. I was trying to live two lives at the same time. One life was about selling dope to a certain crowd, and the other life was trying to do all the right actions to convince a different crowd that I was doing good. I later found out that no one was convinced. I have never been able to do anything halfway; *half measures availed me nothing*. The stinking thinking had returned to my mind, and my primary purpose had become about money once again. I had no spirituality in my life anymore; I had stopped praying entirely. It wasn't that I stopped believing in God, but I was sure he stopped believing in me.

My biggest selling pills were the OC's (oxycontin). I was never prescribed the OC40s or the OC80s, but I had lots of people in my world now. Some needed to sell pills, and some needed to buy pills; it was just about connecting the dots. I was a true middleman. The difference between the oxycodone and the oxycontin was that oxycodone was to treat pain from an injury or from surgery, and oxycontin was for longer lasting pain like from a long-term disease, usually cancer.

In like 2011 or 2012, they pretty much stopped making OC's because of the abuse. See, all one had to do to get rid of the time release in an OC was to scrape it off of the outside of the pill. But then they started making a pill called the OP that had the time release in the whole pill, not just the outside. When that happened, my Roxy sales just became more than I could handle.

Heroin was always one of my biggest fears because of the way it made me feel. I felt a great big incredible surety that everything was going to be alright, no other drug made me feel that way. The fear came from being in love with the feeling. Because of how good it made me feel, I had only shot heroin four of five times in my entire using days, up until then. So that was the feeling I thought I was going to get when I started shooting up again. I never did get that secure feeling that I once got from shooting heroin ever again. Maybe something changed in the drug, or maybe I had just become a different person. Anyway, it was a business decision I made, or that's what I keep telling myself. I could eat or snort five Roxy to kill my pain or I could sell five Roxy's for one hundred dollars and buy a $20 bag of heroin and kill the same pain and have $80 left over; it just made sense.

Just before I switched over to selling heroin, I went broke and I had no money for rent. So I had to move out of that cute little house that Sheryl and I had found. I really had nowhere to go, so my mother told me that I could stay in her condo, and she was gone most the year anyway. My mom loved to stay in Hawaii with my sister, Josie, her husband, Terry, and their three boys—Hayden, Nate, and Dresen.

I stayed at my mom's condo for free. I started to become a real mooch. I stopped attending my 12-step meetings. I had to take a train and two buses to get there, too much trouble. I could feel myself becoming the self-seeking pig dog that didn't need to work on myself anymore. I took off in my head, the money and the drugs made me feel powerful and important, and I did keep selling my pills while I lived at my mom's.

*****

Today is the first day of May. Tomorrow at midnight, I get off of lockdown, thank God. This lockdown is known as full restriction—no visits, no commissary, no television, and no telephone. I get out one hour every other day to walk around the pod and go outside in the fifteen-by-fifty-foot yard, surrounded by thirty-foot walls with a steel gate as a roof. The best part of going outside is looking up at the sky, which has been blue lately. I sure hope I get more mail today.

Eric, a guy who has asked me to work the steps with him, just came up to my cell door and told me goodbye; that's nice, he's getting out. He was here when I got here. He remembered me from the Alano Club where his parents used to take him when he was growing up. He was now done with his fourth step. I wish I could get out of this cell to do his fifth step with him before he goes, but I'm sure he'll find someone on the outs to do it with. I can't wait to attend my weekly AA meeting with Charlie. The guard just brought the mail; I got three letters—one from Sara, one from my mom, and one from my friends, the Paytons.

*****

I was arrested in early 2012 when I pulled into a credit union parking lot. Cozy's girlfriend, Gentri, jumped in my car and bought two Roxy's from me, then jumped out of the car. Just an average stop, nothing different than any of the five stops I had already made that day. After she got out of my car, I pulled up a bit, then backed into a parking spot. I then pulled about fifty or so $20 bills out of my pocket and proceeded to count them on my lap, placing them in certain piles for certain destinations. Because of the amount of dope that was always in my system, and because counting twenties is kind of boring, I nodded off.

I was abruptly wakened by a sharp tap on my window! I opened my eyes to see a cop banging his badge on my driver's side window. When I rolled my window down, the plain clothes detective said, "I think I just saw a drug deal happen. What's that money for and what's in your pockets?"

I said, "We are in a bank parking lot, most people are here for money."

I could tell by the look on his face that he didn't appreciate my trying to make him look dumb. He then asked me again what was in my pockets. I put my hand in one pocket and pulled out my pill bottle with my name on it, full of my Roxy's. I then put my hand into my other pocket and pulled out my sixteen-year AA medallion and my pocket knife with a three-inch blade. He then asked me for my driver's license. So I pulled out my wallet and retrieved my license for him.

He started to walk away but then said, "Stay here, I'll be right back."

I knew I had no warrants, so I wished he'd hurry up, I had places to go. When he did return, he didn't give me back my license. Instead, he said, "Mr. H get out of the car."

I remained sitting there and said, "What the hell? I have no warrants!"

He opened my door and pulled me out of the car, then cuffed me and set me on the hood.

Apparently, this detective, just by chance, was sitting in that credit union parking lot. He had finished his banking and was just about ready to leave and go about his day when he saw me pull in and observed Gentri jump in and out of my car so quickly. He then watched me park and fall asleep. So I guess his keen detective skills knew something was afoot. He said to me, "I called your name in and you're right, you have no warrants, but Mr. H, I see that you are an ex-convict and you have a weapon on you."

I said, "You must be fucking joking, I've carried that little pocket knife around for ten years now and have never had a problem."

He replied, "You may not have a problem now, but it gives me the right to search your vehicle."

He knew he had seen a drug deal, but because the woman he saw get in and out of my car was gone and the Roxy's were in a bottle with my name on it, he had no reason to arrest me. He just hoped that he found something in the car to get me with.

Earlier that day, I had given Luther a ride. Luther was my buddy who had moved to South Dakota with his folks. He was back in town for a visit, and I had picked him up at Bubba's a few hours ago and dropped him off uptown. I was supposed to pick him back up and take him to the airport a bit later. He had left his suitcase and his duffel bag in the hatchback of my Subaru. After an hour of searching my car and Luther's bag and suitcase, while I sat handcuffed in the back of his car, the cop told me that he had found four prescription bottles with narcotics in them! Although the bottles all had Luther's name on them, and they were all in Luther's suitcase, I was still taken to jail on a second-degree distribution charge and did twenty-three days before pretrial released me. I ended up taking two class-A misdemeanors, one for the pocket knife and one for "Attempted possession with an attempt to distribute"—what a fucking joke.

They put me on probation with AP&P (Adult Probation & Parole). I had to report there the next morning; my probation officer was a real dick. He certainly didn't like the way my voice sounded and he was absolutely furious when I informed him that I was prescribed three-hundred Oxycodone 30s every month. He told me, "On a UA, I can't tell the difference between the prescribed oxycodone and heroin!"

I apologized for the pain I was causing him and told him I'd see him next month. The following month, I returned to AP&P for my scheduled appointment. I went in and stood in line but didn't see the dick anywhere. When it was my turn in line, I went up and gave them my appointment card that I was given the month before. I was then informed about all the changes that had happened and to please have a seat until my name was called.

Thirty-five minutes later, I was told that I would be contacted by my probation officer in the next few days. What a waste of my time; oh well, a few days later, I was called by my new PO about five minutes before he arrived at my mom's condo! It was fine; we had a friend over named Patrick who wouldn't shut the fuck up. He was way high on crystal or some kind of speed anyway, but Sara and I handled it just fine. My new PO's name was Mark, and he was very cool and laid back. I quickly apologized about my voice; he said my voice was fine. He then went through the condo room by room, checking for drugs and alcohol to no avail. He then told me that he would call me in the next few days to schedule our next time to meet. We then shook hands, and he left. Things with Mark went fine. He didn't even require me to come into his office every month. I just had to call on the phone and talk with him.

After I was on probation for about nine months, I met a guy named Jim. I'm not really sure how or through whom I knew him; I just did. Jim had a scam where he would write fake prescriptions and pass them off to me. The name on the script wasn't mine. I just played the part of a good friend with a valid identification and picking up a script for someone in so much pain that they couldn't leave the house. I would then get the Roxy's, sell the Roxy's, and give Jim half the profit. It was a good scam, and we made a lot of bank until we had hit all the big pharmacies in Salt Lake County. We could never hit the same pharmacy twice.

Utah County sits just south of Salt Lake County, and I had a lady friend; well, I thought she was a friend. She lived in Utah County but would always drive up to me for her pills. One night, I sent her with three scripts to drop off at three different large pharmacies in Utah County. She came back the next day with some guy driving to take me down to the pharmacies to pick up the pills. I didn't know this guy driving, but I didn't care; I didn't have a car or a license.

We hit the first two pharmacies fine and I had 600 oxycodone pills in my pocket. We arrived at the third pharmacy, and I went in; everything seemed to be the same. When I came out, my lady friend said that she was needed at home and that her mom was on the way to the Walmart where we were to pick her up. She then told me that her friend would drive me home. I gave her twenty of the 900 Roxy's that I now had and hugged her goodbye. As we started to pull away, I asked this guy if he would stop at the gas station so I could by some smokes. After we stopped, he pulled east out of the gas station when the freeway back to Salt Lake was north. I asked him why he was going this way, and he assured me it was a shortcut.

He turned a corner into a subdivision, then pulled into a church parking lot and stopped his truck. He then reached behind him and pulled out a gun, and he stuck it in my side, just below my ribs! This guy demanded that I give him all of my Roxy's! I told him, "No." I then said, "If I show up with no pills, my partner will make me wish I were dead!"

After we argued for a bit, I knew he wasn't going to shoot me, and I think he knew that I knew, so he pulled my head down into his lap and started beating me on the back of my head with the butt of his gun! He kept slamming that gun to the back of my head over and over until I finally said, "Here, you fuck!" and pulled the three prescription bottles out of my pocket and handed them over. He then grabbed my eyeglasses off the floor by his feet and threw them out the window. I jumped out of the passenger side door, and he took off. I tried to read his license plate number, but with no glasses on, I was unable too. I walked over to where he had thrown my glasses and looked until I found them.

I walked out to the street, and the first car that came by stopped. I wasn't sure why. I mean, I could feel the blood running down my back but didn't realize my face was covered. The guy driving the car ran over to me and said, "Are you okay?"

I said, "No."

He then called an ambulance for me as I lay down on the grass on the side of the road and lit up a cigarette. The back of my head was still bleeding so bad that the guy who had stopped said he was getting concerned, but then the ambulance arrived, then the police. As they cleaned the back of my head and got me into the ambulance, I told the police about this guy who jumped me in the church parking lot. I said, "I was just walking through the church parking lot when a little truck pulled up and this guy jumped out and wacked me in the back of the head then stole my money and drove away." I didn't know what to say; it was kind of true.

I was taken to a little hospital in American Fork, which is a little town in Utah County. I called Sara, and she was going to find somebody to come down and pick me up. The doctor put four staples in the back of my head and told me to return in a week to have them removed. Teddy, my daughter, and her boyfriend, Dan, showed up soon to pick me up. On the drive home, I began to think about what I was going to say to Jim. He was going to want his cut. I owed Jim $1,500 for the scripts, and the only way he would forgive a debt was if you got busted and went to jail. He wouldn't care about the staples in my head. I told him that I would get him paid ASAP; I was good to my word, and he was entirely paid back within a month.

A few months later, it was the last part of April 2012, and I was running with this cat, and he was a friend of Jim's and he was my ride to some different pharmacies. We had dropped a few scripts off at a few different pharmacies on the east side of the Salt Lake valley. We had tried to pick one up, but the pharmacist told me that they were unable to verify the doctor who wrote the script. We were then heading back to a grocery store where we had dropped off a script at the pharmacy inside when we noticed a couple of cop cars parked out front. We weren't sure why there were cops parked there, so we parked across the street and waited for them to leave.

We waited for about twenty minutes for them to leave, and when they did, we were on it. He drove to the parking lot on the west side of the store and let me out. I walked into the store just as normal as can be and got into the line at the pharmacy pickup window. When it was my turn, I asked for Greg Peck's prescription, then I said, "I'm a friend of his picking it up for him."

I was told by the lady at the pharmacy window, "Please hold on a moment, you can sit in that chair while we finish it." She then pointed to a chair on the side of the pharmacy.

I don't know, maybe it was the mechanics of her face or just the tone of her voice, but it sounded too rehearsed. I took about three steps toward the chair, then turned toward the exit of the store and began to leave. Two Unified Police Officers grabbed me, one on each side, and they proceeded to walk me outside of the store and place me in the front seat of the police SUV. One of the cops then got in and drove me to jail.

When I got to the jail, they went through my property. I had about $800 cash in my pocket. When I was in booking, waiting to pose for my mug shot, I saw up on the digital board, "Bail Bonds." So I called them and told them how much I had on my books, then told them if I could bail out, please do so, knowing I wouldn't be able to call them after I got dressed in. I then called Sara and told her about my exciting day. She ragged at me and told me she had a bad feeling about all the phony scripts that we'd been doing in Salt

Lake. She said, "It's too saturated here in the valley." She then started to cry. I told her goodbye, and then I was taken for my photo and fingerprinting and dressed in.

The next morning, about two hours after breakfast, I heard a cop yell, "Darren, roll up!" Oh, those famous three words that I've only heard about six times in my life. The words that make me absolutely thrilled no matter what else tragic is happening in my mind. So I did exactly that. I threw my cup, my towel, my toothbrush, and my two sheets onto my blanket that was lying spread out on my bed. Then I "rolled up" the sides of the blanket with all my stuff in the middle and threw it on my back and walked the fuck out of C3 pod of quarantine.

When I walked to the Maverick gas station down the street from the jail, I only had $100 left on me; the bail bond cost me $700. The battery was dead in my cell phone, so I had to use a pay phone to let Sara know that someone had to come for me. Within an hour, I was back at my mom's condo, snorting Roxy's.

Three days later on the second of May, Mark, my probation officer called me on my cell phone. He said, "The West Jordan Judge that put you on probation is mad as hell that you're not in jail and has issued two $15,000 warrants for your arrest." Then he said, "I'll be over in an hour to take you back to jail."

That sure was nice of him to do. He certainly didn't need to warn me like that. I knew he was a good guy. One hour was all I had to get ready for who knows how long. Sara and I were fighting about something, so she was up at a girlfriend's house. I called Kyra in South Jordan for a ride to the store. I told her that I'd sell her ten Roxy 30s for fifteen bucks a piece, which saved her $50 from the regular price. She was there in fifteen minutes. We then drove to the grocery store. Once outside of the store, I said, "I'm running in for a rib eye steak, will you please go next door to the 7-Eleven and buy a condom?" Then I winked at her and gave her $5.

On the short drive back to the condo, I told that beautiful Kyra that the condom wasn't for sex and that I would never mask the feeling of being inside her with a latex wall. Kyra had always been a very good, very beautiful, and very married customer. When we got back to my mom's condo, I sold her the ten pills and told her goodbye.

Once I was back at home, I of course called Sara and tried to work out our fight. I told her about the call from Mark, my PO, and that I had a steak on the grill and a condom to pack for my adventure! I opened a can of corn and made up a green salad to go with my rib eye. When I finished my meal, I packed for my trip. Since toiletries and clothes aren't allowed in jail, I packed the only thing I could, which was that condom. I packed it with thirty Roxy 30s, thirty Soma's, and fifteen OC 80s that I'd been saving for a special occasion; this seemed special enough. I then tried to relax and went into the bathroom and sat down. Once I was empty, I put some lotion on that pill-packed condom and inserted it into my bum. I then jumped in and out of the shower real fast. It had almost been an hour since Mark called.

I hurried and called Sara and told her I was going now and that I'd call her from booking. Then I said, "Please get me out as soon as you can, and my mom will be back on May 10, so if you can't get me out by then, please clean the condo."

The ride to the jail was pleasant. I wasn't even cuffed. Mark and I talked about my new charge. I played stupid. I told him, "I was just grabbing a script for a friend of mine. I didn't know it was phony."

His response was, "Well, the judge wants you down a little bit longer." We got there and I got booked in and then called Sara, and then I was dressed and went back to quarantine where I stayed for nine days. I hate the food in jail. All I can usually eat is the pudding and Jell-O. I knew that the more I ate, the faster I would have to use the bathroom so the quicker I would get my drugs. It took about twelve hours to get that condom out of me, but once out, the nine days in quarantine flew right by, I think; I don't really remember.

Sara came by for visits a couple times, and she told me they were nice visits, but I seemed a bit out of it. On day nine, they moved me from quarantine to Section D, minimum security, and I was there about two hours, and then I heard those famous words, "Darren, roll up!"

As I started my walk down the long jailhouse hallway, I could certainly feel that I hadn't walked much over the past nine days. I really started to dread that long walk over to the Maverick gas station once I was out of the jail. I was also a bit nervous not knowing who bailed me out or who would come pick me up. As I reached the end of the long hallway and I pushed open the door to the visiting lobby, there sat Cal and Sheri. Cal was the biggest Roxy connection that I had; Sheri was his lady.

Cal got a couple hundred 30s a month, and Sheri got the Roxy 10s. Sheri gave me five 10s as we walked down the ramp to the parking lot; they tasted good as I chewed them up. Cal told me that his mother put up the title to her car to get me out but that they had no choice. Cal then said, "It's been miserable trying to make money without you and your clientele, Darren!"

My ego sure liked hearing those words, but two $15,000 warrants meant $3,000 is what they had to put up to get me out. Let the games begin!

My mom had been back a couple of days now. Sara had failed to clean the condo like I asked her to. The condo was a real mess, and my mom is a clean freak, so I was not invited back. I asked Cal and Sheri if I could stay with them for a few days. They told me, "Sure, of course." It was known by all that I would be working nonstop! I called my Sara who came over immediately, and we went to work selling all of Cal and Sheri's Roxy's in two days, and they were gone! Then I called my Iranian Roxy connections that always had however many I wanted for $15 apiece. Sara, who went to the same pain clinic as I, told me that because of my arrest for trying to use a forged script, I had been cut off from the clinic. I called the clinic to verify, and sure enough, I was told that my pain doctor didn't want me to come back!

The next day, Sara was at the movies with her kids, and I needed fifty Roxy 30s that she had. So I texted her and made her come out of the theater to meet me; she was so mad! I had been going so hard since I was bailed out of jail I had forgotten to sleep. I had not done any crystal meth since I got out. It was just pure adrenaline keeping me going and my determination to get Cal's mom paid back. I don't remember who drove me over to the theater to meet Sara, but I do remember being on Cal and Sheri's couch, and that's the last thing I do remember.

When I awoke and there was something stuck in my throat, I thought, *What the fuck?* I tried to speak, and no words came out. Then I saw my mom sitting next to the bed. I had no idea where I was! I couldn't speak, so I clapped my hands together to get my mom's attention. Then I pointed to my face and mouthed the words, "What the fuck!"

My mom, who could speak just fine, explained to me that the contraption in my throat was to help me breath. She then told me they tried to remove it yesterday but you couldn't get any air. She looked at me, puzzled, like I should know what she was talking about, but she could tell by my expression I had no clue. I motioned my hand like I was writing, so Mom got in her purse and retrieved a pen, then got into the drawer by the bed for a notebook. She handed both items to me. I wrote, "Why am I here? Is Sara and Teddy okay?"

She shook her head yes and said, "Teddy and Barbie-Momma are on their way down."

I grabbed the notebook again and wrote, "What happened to me?"

She told me that she wasn't sure and that Cal and Sheri called the ambulance because they couldn't get me to wake up. She then said, "When the ambulance arrived, you were in a coma, and that was four days ago."

It was nice having Teddy Bear and her mom there. The last time the three of us were in an ICU together, Teddy was in Barbie's tummy, growing fingers and toes and stuff. My baby girl told me that the doctors thought this was a suicide attempt. I moved my hands back and forth in a "why" motion.

She said, "Because of all drugs you have in your system." She then hugged me real tight and said, "I love you."

I grabbed the notebook and wrote, "You know I would never kill myself, right? That's just what's in my blood most the time. I snorted some oxy-cotton 80s in jail the other day and I've been on the 30s nonstop since I got out and had no food but jailhouse Jell-O and pudding every couple days and a little bit of salad." Then I wrote, "I had a very hard time sleeping in jail, even though I was so high.

Oxycodone and oxycontin and any painkiller that's not got an acetaminophen base, after a while, taking it no longer makes you tired but actually amps you up."

The next day, the doctor came in and told me, "You threw up in your lung (aspirated), and that caused your lung to shut down. The lack of oxygen to your brain caused your coma." He then told me he wasn't sure why I was still alive. He then said, "I'll take that out of your throat, but you'll have to wear a breathing contraption on your face." I immediately nodded my head yes, then put my hands together like I was praying. He then left and returned in about ten minutes with two ladies and a guy.

The doctor put this tool down my throat and pulled out a peculiar shaped contraption. My first words were, 'Thank you." My seconds words were, "Water, please give me some water." My third words were, "Man, do I sure need a cigarette!"

I was told "No!" by everyone.

I was in the ICU for a week with lots of visitors every day. Before I left, the doctor came in to talk to me. He said, "You're the only person I've ever met who has lived through two comas. You won't make it through a third." He then told me to be careful and that I would be on the oxygen for a while.

*****

Writing and thinking about what was different after my second coma, one thing that I and am sure of and many others noticed was that I drooled quite often. I think maybe my face is a little more numb then it was from my traumatic brain injury back in 1987. I really had no idea where I was going when the cop yelled those magical words, "Darren, roll up!" But then he said, "You're moving sections," which killed the magic. So I rolled all my commissary, all my papers and books and everything up in my blanket, and stuffed it in the seat of my wheelchair, then pushed my chair out to the guard station.

The guard said, "Just wait in the multipurpose room because of your write up. Your matrix is too high, so you have to move to medium security."

When I arrived in medium security pod 1A, the guards made me empty everything out of my blanket onto the floor. Then he took all of my noodles, my coffee cup, and my bowl, and he said, "You can't have those in medium." He then told me, "You be credited back on your commissary for those Top Ramen noodles." He then said, "This cup and bowl will just grow mold on them as they sit in property, would you like me to throw them away?"

I could tell that the guard just didn't want to do the work of wrapping up the bowl and cup and putting them in property. So I said, "Yes, sir, I definitely want to keep those items." *Fuck that lazy punk!* I was so mad that the guard over in D pod didn't tell me about the restrictions in medium. I would have loved to leave my seven bags of noodles and my cup and bowl with my broke ass celli in D pod.

Things are very different over here in medium. The top tier and the bottom tier don't get out at the same time. It's really kind of fucked up here. The segregation is certainly not politically correct. They've got all the brothers and most everyone that's not white on the top tier, and they have me with my disability on the ground floor with all the peckerwoods. If it makes it safer and more controllable, well, fine, but it means that we have to be locked down every other day. Having that damn pill in my pocket was the worst mistake I ever made. Thank God I have court in the morning so I can get out of this cell for half the day anyway.

*****

Sara only came once to the hospital to see me. My mom was so mad at Sara for not cleaning up our disaster we left in her condo. My mom also blamed Sara for my overdose. After about a week in the ICU at Pioneer Valley Hospital, I was able to wheel myself downstairs to smoke; nobody would help me. Two days later, I was cleared to go home. My mom let me stay at her place, but not Sara. Cal and

Sheri had kept my cell phone to have all my customers phone numbers—pretty fucked up! Most of my people told them to fuck off when they called, but I did lose a few good customers.

I lived at my mom's for a couple weeks and then moved into a place over by my big sister's. The place I moved to was a thirty-room apartment building for men, and rent was only $300 a month. Having an income of $700 from SSI made it possible for me to live there. Mom was happy that I had a safe place to live. She was only here for a short time, and then back to Hawaii she went. I lived there for a couple months, but the rules there made it hard. I couldn't have guests over after 9:00 p.m., and once my traffic picked back up, I had to move on.

While I was there, I met a guy who was hanging out at the store on the corner. His name was Clyde. Clyde, or as Sara and I ended up calling him, "Kearns Clyde," introduced us to Kevin and Cory. Kevin sold heroin, lots and lots of heroin. Being cut off from the pain clinic and my oxycodone made my relationship with Kevin very lucrative. I can't count the number of customers that made the switch from those expensive Roxy's over to the cheap heroin. They just needed the inspiration that came when I told them it was all I sold now. I started shooting heroin and I always did too much, which caused me to overdose a lot. Thank God it was never enough to kill me.

Kevin and Cory and their daughter, Hailey, lived in a house that they rented about a mile east of my mom's condo. They asked me if I'd like to move in and share the upstairs with Hailey. They told me that the money would really help them out, and since I needed a place to go, it was perfect for a few months. I moved a lot of black and crystal and medical marijuana through that house. Then one day, the guy who owned the house that we were renting asked us to move out. Kevin and Cory threw a fit. I didn't really care. I was making so much money slinging three different kinds of dope. Living at a motel was probably safer for me anyway. I found that with the amount of traffic I had, I had to change motels every week. The motels would ask me to.

After a few months of jumping from motel room to motel room, Sara got so tired of it that she moved into a motel room with

Kevin and Cory's daughter, Hailey. I was asked to not bring any trouble their way. Kevin and Cory lived in a motor home. Now they would just park it in big parking lots at night to sleep. I got real tired of the fast-paced life of not having a home. Finally, after I was ripped off twice and then robbed at gunpoint, I was ready for a break. My mom was back from Hawaii, so I went there and asked if I could stay for a while. She missed me, so she let me crash over there for a while, but it didn't take long until I was back doing hotels every night with Sara.

Sara and I got arrested after leaving a hotel one morning. We were pretty broke; dope was almost gone and we were walking through the McDonald's parking lot. I said something rude to Sara, and she hit me with my cane. Some nosey Nelly thought it was her duty to call the police, and as she drove by us, she yelled out the window, "The police are coming!" I heard the word *police,* and I moved as fast as I could over the small grassy knoll behind the McDonald's and slid my body through the empty space where there was a missing piece of the wood fence. I pulled out of my pocket a few grams of pot and the smidgen of go-fast I had left. I placed my dope under a rock beneath a bush and spied up at Sara talking to the cops. She didn't have any drugs on her, so what could the problem be? I really thought that going back up that little grassy hill to where Sara was would be the knightly thing to do. I was sure that I just needed to tell the police that the lady that called was crazy and that Sara never swung my cane at me.

Before I could get to where Sara was, another police car pulled up to me, and a cop jumped out and said, "Can I please see some identification?"

I gave him my state ID, and he got back in his car while I stood there and stared over at my Sara. About five minutes later, he jumped back out of his car, walked over to me, and said, "You have three warrants for your arrest!"

I guess that sounded about right. I had kept missing court dates in Taylorsville on a stupid little "driving on suspension" ticket I got a few months back, plus I hadn't paid the county probation fees in a few months. He cuffed me and read me my rights and put me in the front seat of his car. Then he walked over to the car where Sara was sitting in the back and grabbed a bag out of the front seat. The police officer then came back over to me and sat down in the driver's seat. I could now see that the bag in his hand had a familiar white box in it. I knew that in that white box were four ten-pack bags of hypodermic needles. He then said, "She says these are yours."

My first reaction was, of course, to deny, but I remembered telling Sara that we needed to always keep her name clean, so if you ever get popped, say it was me. So she had done what I had asked her to do, and along with going to jail on warrants, I also had a new paraphernalia beef for the needles.

I did nine days in jail and did one video court hearing and one in person hearing. I don't remember any withdrawal; it actually felt like I was on break, like a vacation. After my last hearing, I got out, and it was pretty early in the morning when I finally hit the streets. My mother was the only one I knew who would be awake and willing to come get me.

After she picked me up, our first stop was where I was arrested. I climbed back through the fence, and my dope was where I left it. I was happy. Next, we stopped over to Sara's parent's house. It was nice to see her. Sara and I now had court dates, mine for paraphernalia and hers for disturbing the peace. Hers came first, and she got a fine and some community service hours. The judge told her that when she paid her fine and worked her hours, he would clear it off her record. I also got a fine and some hours to work off, but my fine was waived for a while because of my disability.

The following month, I was arrested again; well, not really arrested but charged with a crime. One night, I got dropped off at Denny's to meet some people who wanted some black, and I ended up waiting for hours for these people. My cell phone was dead, so although I had access to a pay phone, all my numbers were in my cell. I ended up falling asleep on the floor by the pay phone and waking up on a stretcher, hearing a cop telling the manager that they were taking me to the IHC hospital. I reached my hand down to my pocket to feel for the eight-ball of heroin that I brought to sell, and it was not there! I remembered nothing else until the next morning I awoke in a hospital bed.

I had scanners taped to my chest that I could see my hands and arms were coved by a blanket. I knew that my wrists were covered to hide the silver bracelets that the cops carry. I was also sure there was an IV in my arm. As I lifted my hand up to hear the metal on metal clanging sound, there was none! No IV either. I looked over to the side of the bed and saw my clothes and my shoes were on the floor. I reached over and grabbed my jeans, then looked in the pocket for my cell phone, and it was there; still dead but there. I got dressed and walked out of that hospital room. There was a nurse outside the door at the station. I said to her, "Am I good to go?"

She said, "Sure."

So I walked down the hallway until I saw a hospital phone. I called my mom to get Sara's cell number. I called Sara and told her about my night, then asked her to find me a ride. I then walked out of the hospital to smoke and wait for—well, who knows who?

Randy pulled up about twenty minutes later. "The ride," Randy said, "will cost you a twenty bag, and I have $20, so I need a forty bag."

I said, "I have no black, bro, I think the cops took it."

He yelled and threw his usual fit. So I told him to drive me over to my guy's house and I'd give him a sixty for that $20.00 he had in his pocket. This made my puppet, Randy, happy as pie.

The following week, like four or five days later, I was driving one of Kyle's cars that I went with him to pick up. He told me to just keep the car for the night. I was down at the Executive Inn Hotel in West Valley. It was about 1:00 a.m. I had just met up with Kevin and scored a twenty bag. I was out and couldn't re-up until the next day. After I scored, I drove to the back of the hotel and parked. I scooted over to the passenger side of the car. I had my arm tied off and a flashlight between my teeth, trying to find a vein. I looked over and saw a police spotlight flash from the corner of the hotel. So I put my head down by my knees so they wouldn't see me.

I sat and listened. I could hear the car stop and the door open, and then I could hear them walking outside the car, so I didn't move. All of a sudden, the passenger door opened up! The cop said, "What are you doing?" He then shone his flashlight at my tied off arm; his question then became rhetorical. He shone his flashlight down by my feet and saw a spoon halfway filled with a heroin and water mix and a little piece of cotton. He said, "Don't kick that over!"

So I did. The car was so old and messy that they could never get anything testable off that carpet in that front seat. The needle had a bunch of my blood in it because I had found a vein but then pulled out because I couldn't see. The cop was so damn mad because they found me with a bloody needle and a tie around my arm, so they had to call an ambulance! When the ambulance arrived, they took my vitals. Then the cop asked me, "Do you want to go to jail or the hospital?"

Once again with the rhetorical, this cop was a hoot. I then said, "Hospital, please."

The cop laughed and then they put me on a stretcher and into the ambulance, then off to the hospital we went. We were too far west to go to the big IHC hospital, so we went to the Pioneer Valley Hospital. When I awoke, this time uncuffed, I wasn't so shocked. I had called Sara the night before when I was dropped off by the police, so she was on a bus headed to me. I met her at the bus stop, and we walked up the street to some shade to wait for someone to call in need so we could get a ride to score some dope.

Sara was now living in a little trailer parked out back of the duplex where Kevin and Cory were living. Kevin owed Sara a lot of money that she paid him for a lot of Roxy's that he never got, so the deal was that she could live in the spare room in the duplex, rent-free, until he made it right. Hailey, their daughter, needed a place to live, so Sara offered to live in the trailer out back. Now Hailey was also pregnant, and her boyfriend and his two little girls shared the room with Hailey.

My staying with Sara in that little trailer was causing problems. The biggest problem was all my traffic. A lot of times, I would walk up the street to meet people, but still, it was noticeable. Thursday, the twelfth of September 2013, I was out of dope and money! In the past two or so years of selling heroin, I had only run out once. I got so sick I swore to God I would never run out again! And I didn't, but now I was out again. The problem was that I had to slow my traffic way down, but the amount that Sara and I used didn't slow at all. I wasn't going to suffer like I did last time I ran out, so I told Sara I was done and I could not come off the cheese again! So I called my big sister, Kimberly, and begged her to come and take me to the hospital!

She said, "Of course, Darren, I'll be right there."

My sister took me to the University of Utah Hospital where they checked me over and then sent me to the Ogden Regional Hospital for insurance reasons. When we arrived, my sister went in with me to look around, then told me she loved me and took off. I was taken to a room by a man and asked a hundred questions. We then walked down a long hall and into a room with a bed. I was given a gown and told by a nurse, "I'll be right back with some Librium and Suboxone."

For three days, I was at that hospital, shaking and aching and coming down. They sent me home with a one-week supply of the Suboxone. I was to take a full 8-mm strip a day for three days, then half a strip for two days, and a quarter of a strip for two days. Then I was done. Coming off Suboxone is not a lot of fun either, but I did it. My sister, Kimberly, let me stay at her place for a while. My mom was back in Hawaii, so I couldn't stay there. She wouldn't be back for a month. I needed to get a place to live, but my family thought I needed treatment. I hunted for an intensive outpatient program with the help of my sister. I only had a few days until my scheduled appointment with the county probation, which was ordered by the Midvale judge for the paraphernalia charge I got that day with Sara.

When I was last on probation, they had ordered me to an IOP (Intensive Out Patient) called Clinical Consultants, but I never went. This place was run by a man named Santiago. I knew him from 1996 when I paroled to Odyssey House. He was the man in charge of Odyssey, and I considered him a friend. I had called Clinical Consultants and made an appointment with a man named Heber. Heber was to do an assessment to see if I needed treatment, and if so, the state would pay for it.

I met Heber and he was very cool. I told him that I desperately needed a bed in a treatment center. I then told him my sister was great but she couldn't support me. Heber told me that he thought I was cool. He then told me that his assessment on me will say anything I wanted it to.

The following day, I went to county probation, which by the way is not as intense as the state AP&P was. I met with a lady who told me she would not be my probation officer. She was just there to get me started. She asked me a bunch of questions and then said she must send me elsewhere to be assessed. I told her I was assessed yesterday at Clinical Consultants. She said, "Perfect, that will work just fine." She then had me sign a release of information that she could fax over to clinical and then set up an appointment to come back a month later and meet my new probation officer. Her name was Joel D.

*****

Today, here in medium security, the lower tier got p.m. out of lockdown, and tomorrow, we'll have a.m. out. We play a lot of poker here in jail for commissary items, which is nice. Today at 3:00, I asked the guard to change the channel on the TV to my program, which is Law & Order SVU. Watching Olivia Benson can turn a bad day into a good one. I love her with all my heart. This evening, I talked to my mom and to my dad. They both told me that my grandma H was not doing well and she was the last living grandparent I had. She was ninety-seven years old and swam laps at the pool every day. She just stopped swimming a couple years back. Her memory was pretty bad but as far as I could tell, that was the only thing different about her. She was the cutest grandma ever, always so kind and giving, just like Grandpa H was.

****

I lived with my sister, Kimberly, until my mom got back from Oahu, then I moved back in with my mom. We immediately started looking for a place for me to move to. We looked and looked on the Internet, and we would find places, but something was always just off. Then a place came up just around the corner from my sister Kimberly's house, which was only about a mile from my mom's condo. It was a room in a three-story house, and it was the master bedroom. It was a huge room, and there was just one other tenant in the basement, but I had a total of nine roommates. I immediately paid the landlord the rent of $450 and the $200 deposit. That was on the sixth of December 2013.

It took me a while to get all of my belongings, which were in a storage area, moved over to my master bedroom, but I did. I or we got everything I owned and that Sara owned into that bedroom. Once Tony, my new landlord, learned that I had a live-in girlfriend, my rent went up $100, and so did the deposit. Sara knew as well as I that there was no way I could pay $550 a month for rent when I only received $700 a month from SSI. Sara was in no shape to get a job to help out. She was still pretty strung out on the heroin. She had slowed down a lot since I had stopped, and she would never fix in front of me, but we both knew she was still on it and couldn't work a job. My decision to keep selling heroin wasn't really a choice per se, but it was my only option. It was either put Sara and I in a minimum wage job, flipping burgers at some fast-food joint where I would lose my SSI benefits, which also meant I would lose my food stamps and medical benefits, just so we could pay rent; or I could be a heroin dealer who didn't use heroin. It seemed like a pretty easy decision at the time.

I was living life on life's terms. I started to attend Clinical Consultants four times a week as ordered by the courts or by probation. I was required to call every night after 9:00 p.m. and find out the color for the next day. If it was my color, that meant I had to go in and give a urinalysis before 6:00 p.m.

Shortly after my classes in IOP started, I hooked up with an old buddy who sold black tar heroin. My main heroin dealer sold me a brown powder heroin. Both were equally as good; they were just different. I had customers who would only buy the brown and others the black, so having both was just good business. I also started moving the weed and the go-fast because of the large demand for both. Living in a house with nine roommates and Sara, all of whom were on one kind of drug or another, had its ups and downs. Two of the ladies on the top floor would usually buy a gram a day of the medical marijuana, and the brother and sister on the same floor loved the crystal meth and the brown cheese.

There was only one room on ground floor. The guy who occupied that room and Sara became very good friends. I liked the friendship because it gave Sara something to do, someone for her to hang out with because I was gone most the time, working. Sara's friend, whose name was Royce, didn't do heroin, and that was a good thing for my Sara. Royce and Sara loved to smoke the meth, though.

My heroin dealers changed over time for one reason or another. Kevin and Cory were pretty small-time; that just meant buying from them was more expensive. James, who I actually met when I was living with Kevin and Cory, was a bit cheaper for the same quality of heroin. He was my most visited connection until he ripped me off. James overdosed on heroin, and that's hard to do when you're only a smoker, like James was. One must smoke a lot of black to overdose, but he did. I was James' biggest customer, and that was kind of a bad thing because the black that he had was profit made by selling me a half ounce every day, and his mother knew. His mom was in the game as well, but the scared look in her eyes at the hospital that day I will never forget.

After he got out of the hospital, we talked about recovery and doing meetings together but never did. Instead, we worked out a way for James to keep half of the heroin that I would buy through him and sell it for me. The next day, I went over to James' house, and he had no heroin and no money either. What he did have was a bullshit story about going to jail and getting busted with my black!

I had taken James over to Russ's house before, and I knew that's where James got his heroin. I even knew that Russ's connection was Chad. We all knew each other from the game and would nod to one another in passing but would never speak because of the code; the rule about stepping on each other's toes is still honored by some of us. When James took six grams of my heroin and had no money to show for it, it was, to me, a free pass to step all over his fucking toes. The next day, I showed up at Russ's house and knocked on the door. A pretty little baby-doll answered the door.

I asked, "Is Russ home? I'm Darren."

She told me to hold on and shut the door, leaving me on the porch. She came back about a minute later and said, "He's in the kitchen."

I walked in the house and through the front room. I noticed three kids in the corner. Two must have been about five years old and the third about six months old. I kept walking the only way I could, which was down the hall. The hallway ended in the kitchen, and there was Russ, sitting at the table. I said, "Hey, man, I'm Darren."

He said, "Yes, I know. I was wondering when you would get tired of being fucked by James."

I told him, "I didn't mind my bags being a little short. He needed to keep himself well each day, but this time he straight out lied to me!" I then told him about my giving James half of the quarter ounce that I bought yesterday for him to sell and how he told me he got popped with it. His laughter confirmed my knowing that James was a fat-mouthed liar. I came right out and asked Russ if I could come straight to him.

He said, "Of course, most of my customers were once James's."

I bought a half ounce from Russ every three days. A quarter ounce would cost me $300 where a half ounce would only run me $550, so I would save $50. Now Russ lived downtown so I would have to pay someone $10 to pay for gas to get me there and back. I really liked dealing with Russ. He turned out to be one of my favorite people I dealt with. We made a lot of money together; all was well until it wasn't.

On my way to play poker with my sober buddies, I stopped downtown to grab a half ounce from Russ. He and his family had been thrown out of their home, so I met him over at the motel that they were staying at. Russ only had a ball on him, which in the heroin world is three grams. So I paid him for the ball and gave him another $550 on top of that for a half tomorrow. This was no big deal. I floated money to Russ and his wife all the time. The next day, he didn't have my half or my money. He said something about his sister-in-law ripping him off or something like that. I didn't care, I just needed my dope or my money!

I was forced to call Kevin and Cory's neighbor, Brock. I just knew the price would be so high. I went for a ride with Brock who used my cell phone to call his guy who happened to be running late. The deal never happened, and we had to drop Brock back off at home. About a half hour after we dropped Brock off, my cell phone rang. I answered it, and it was Brock's connection asking if Brock was there.

I told him, "No, sorry, man, we had to get the truck we were borrowing back and we had to drop Brock off at home."

The voice on the phone said, "Darren?"

It was Dan on the phone. He was a guy I had known for a couple years. Actually, Sara and I met Dan and his girlfriend the same time we met Kevin and Cory. Kearns Clyde brought the four of them over to my mom's condo back when I was living in that men's apartment complex.

So anyway, Dan told me that I didn't need to use Brock as a middle man and I could come directly to him. I quickly invited him over and told him I needed a half ounce. He arrived about forty minutes later and he charged me six bills for his dope. His heroin was a big black chunk, certainly different than Russ's. I had my Sara try it out. Sara said, "It tastes as good if not better than Russ's dope." This was a good hook-up. I hoped Brock wasn't too bummed out missing the twenty bag he would have made doing the deal.

Some people loved the new black dope and some missed the brown Russ dope. But it was the next morning and I was out of dope, so I called Russ and asked if he had my money yet. He said, "No, but why don't you grab some muscle and meet me over there?"

I said, "Russ, what the fuck are you talking about, homeboy?" Then I said, "If I go anywhere, it will be to where you are. I gave my cake to you man."

It was silent. Now Russ is a hard-ass ex-convict with an old prison number, not quite as old as mine, but he was down quite a bit longer than I, and he was covered in prison ink. He was not used to being talked to the way that I was talking to him, but business is business. I broke the silence by saying, "I will buy Chad's phone number from you for the $550 you owe me."

He didn't say anything for a minute and then rattled off a ten-digit phone number. I said, "Thank you."

I sent Chad a text as soon as I got his number. I had met Chad a few times, and we had looked at each other, both thinking that we should talk but, of course, never did. I first met Chad through James, then later at Russ's house. The politics of selling dope is a bit funny. When I would buy large enough amounts through James, Chad would bring it over. When James would play his stupid little games and I would go elsewhere, then he never needed a large enough amount to bother the big guy. James would just go to Russ for the smaller amounts. When I would buy a full ounce or even a half an ounce, sometimes Chad would be over at Russ's when I got there. So I knew who he was, and he knew that I knew.

It took Chad about forty minutes to text me back. The text said, "Hey, dude, what's up? Russ said you'd be getting a hold of me, whatcha need?"

I texted him back, "A half ASAP."

His text read, "21st and 7th 20 min…$500."

I texted, "Cool, see you in 20."

I called one of my rides, and they were just around the corner. She was with me in five minutes, and we flew up and met Chad. After I had bought five-and-a-half ounces from Chad at my new price, I made back the $550 I had lost from Russ. I could tell by the way the heroin looked that Russ was cutting it a little bit, but whatever. I was now done with the small-time James and I was done with Russ. I was also done with Brock. I now had straight connections to two of the biggest heroin connections in this town.

Most of my customers loved the Russ dope; well, it's now called the Chad dope. I also had a handful of customers who preferred the black tar. So being the pal that I always was to junkies with money, I always had both kinds available. I was so busy selling dope that I forgot about trying to get Sara clean and I forgot about my recovery as well. Clinical Consultants dropped me out of IOP, so I now just had group on Monday and Friday mornings, so I really was doing well as far as doing what the courts wanted and not using drugs.

*****

I'm here in my cell in medium security. It's about 6:15 on Saturday night. Benjamin, my celli, is sleeping and I'm sitting in my wheelchair with the soft cushion seat, writing. I always get a wheelchair when I come to jail because the walk from where the cells are to transportation, a walk that will always happen, is about a hundred yards. It's not that I can't walk that far; it's that I can't walk it fast enough, so it always pisses the guards off. It's also easier to be in a chair when going to court. It gives me access to the elevator.

I was just sitting here, thinking how unfair it is of me to be mad at Sara for being a junkie. I was the one who brought her into this world, into the game of making money, or in her case, making dope for just the profit but just the game of supplying junkies with their needed medicine. I kept her surrounded with the heroin, crystal meth, Roxy's, and with the medical marijuana and expected her to want to get clean with me.

My job was always happening and my time off work was usually between 2:00 a.m. and 9:00 a.m., so that is when I slept and dedicated time to Sara. Sara's job was to weigh out my twenties. I would give her the twelve-gram half ounce each night, and she would make me sixty twenties and put them in a Ziplock that went into my pants pocket. There was something missing from our sex life. I hated to think that in my clean state of mind, maybe I just wasn't attracted to her, but I sure wanted to be. She sat home all day and shot the heroin that I would leave for her. Perhaps I was making her unattractive to me so I would have a reason to get back on the go-fast. It was hard watching her shoot her cheese.

I wanted that sex drive back that I used to have in the nineties up in Portland when I'd shoot the crank made with the P2P chemical for a base; all there was now was crystal meth with an ephedrine base. I needed something to rekindle my sex life or maybe I'm just a junkie; anyway, I started shooting the crystal again. My shooting the go-fast again started real slow. I would only do it once a week at first. I would wait until 9:05 on Friday and call Clinical Consultants and check the color for Saturday. If it wasn't yellow, my color, then that meant I had until Monday at 8:30 p.m. until I might have to give a urine sample. That was plenty of time to have a quarter-gram shot circulate through my system and be out of me.

****

Chad and I made a lot of money together pretty quickly, and I started feeling bad for Russ. I called Russ up and went and met him and his wife. I gave them a couple hundred dollars. They were hurting pretty bad, and it made me feel good to help them out. The next day, we had a commotion at the house. Kearns Clyde came over and he had Brock with him. Now I had never seen those two together before, but I met Kevin and Cory through Kearns Clyde, and I met Brock through Kevin and Cory, so it made sense. They were just a couple of white trash Kearns bums that came over.

Carrie, one of my roommates, started yelling because Clyde walked his bike in through the closed gate into the backyard. He left his bike and Brock in the backyard and came walking in through the side door, then down the stairs, and knocked on my bedroom door. The problem with that is this is a home where people live, and although Clyde didn't do anything wrong, Carrie had a reason to bitch; so she did.

Kearns Clyde, of course, had some kind of electronic gizmo he wanted to trade for some black. I wasn't interested in making a trade with Clyde, but it took so long to get him out of the house. When I finally got him to leave and I walked him up the stairs and outside, I learned that his bike and Brock were in the backyard. As I was getting these two to leave, Kevin M pulled up in the driveway. He was driving his black truck. He always just showed up without calling first and was always hurting but always had a grip of money. I walked to the end of the driveway and jumped into his truck.

The first thing he said as we pulled down the road was, "Is that that fucking Brock?"

I replied, "Yeah, Kearns Clyde brought him over, they were just leaving."

He then rattled off something about getting fucked over on a deal that Brock put together. Kevin then pulled out $160 and asked for two grams. I pulled out my Ziplock and counted out ten twenty sacks for him. Kevin was a fan of the hard-black Dan dope.

Brock called the next day and asked if he could come over for a sixty bag. Knowing how much Sara hated traffic coming over, I told him I would meet him at the market on the corner. Then I took off. It was about a ten-minute walk for me to get down to the market on the corner. After I met Brock and his wife, whom I had never even heard of before, we did our deal, and they ran me back home and dropped me off. I didn't hear back from Brock for two days. I mentioned that I didn't hear back from Brock for two days because it was so odd that I heard from him at all. I mean, he was the one who got me, not on purpose, back in touch with Dan and the black tar. Brock wasn't getting a better deal from me, so I wasn't really sure why I was getting his business, but who cared? His money was as green as everybody else's.

Two days later, he ordered another sixty. I wasn't sure why he ordered another sixty. It was kind of odd. I had people who would buy twenty sacks all day and people who would buy three-gram balls and six-gram quarters, and even a few that would buy grams. People don't usually buy sixty of heroin for $60 because for another $20, I would sell you a gram which is forty more of dope for $20 more. I guess some junkies just aren't too smart.

A few days later, I went to my one-on-one at Clinical, and my therapist, Heber, told me I would have an easier time convincing the rest of the staff to let me graduate if I got a haircut and shaved off my beard. I said, "Okay, I guess we live in a material world, and I am a material girl."

He laughed and said, "Whatever."

I did want a haircut. My hair was a bit long, and I wore a bandana every day because of the length. Sara was all for my haircut, and we thought cutting my hair would get me graduated faster. My probation officer had told me it would just be a couple months after I finished treatment, and she would put in for my completion of probation. So what the hell, I got a haircut. It was kind of nice. The lady that cut my hair used to attend Clinical Consultants, and through speaking with her, I found out she did her one-on-ones with Heber as well. She wrote a message on one of her business cards and asked me to give it to Heber. I told her, "What a small world. Everything has a reason why it happens. The people we meet and the things we do all have a purpose."

She smiled and agreed with me.

The following weekend was very nice. We celebrated St. Patrick's Day at my mother's condo. Sara was invited and accepted. She hadn't been invited by my mom anywhere since my coma in 2012, so it was a blessed event, and I only had to stray away outside to do one drug deal. We had a nice day with lots of food and family. Things were a little strange that week, and I shot more meth in my arm than usual. When I called in on Tuesday, my color came up, so I did a UA on Wednesday. My color had only been coming up once a week lately, so I thought I'd be fine doing another shot that night. I waited until 9:00 p.m. and called in, and it wasn't my color, so I did one and we played all night, then I did another one that next morning.

On Friday, when I called, my color came up. I waited as late as I could on Saturday to do my test and after was told it was dirty for crystal meth amphetamine! I just kind of blew it off because I knew they would have to send it to a lab to get a confirmation that it was really dirty. I started to rack my brain about what kind of story I could come up with on how this wasn't my fault. I thought about saying that someone at my house had it in for me and they must have put some go-fast in my coffee.

On Monday, it was the actual St. Patrick's Day. I went to group, and everyone loved my haircut. Nobody mentioned anything about my dirty UA on Saturday, thank God. The next night was very strange. I had three ladies stop by between 10:00 and 12:00, two for heroin and one for go-fast. It never happens like that. I'll let one stop by every so often, but I really try not to let traffic come by. They all came at separate times and all parked down the road and walked up to the front porch so it wasn't obvious; just a little strange.

Sara and I didn't cuddle that night. We were both just so tired. That was the eighteenth of March 2014, my last night in the life.

*****

The nineteenth of May, day sixty-one in jail, I was taken to court. My attorney assured me that drug court would have reconsidered taking me. I was shipped from the jail with about forty other dark-blue jumpsuit-wearing cats to the courthouse downtown; I was the only one that needed to be pushed in a wheelchair. We were taken off the bus and herded into a big cell, and then ten of us at a time were taken to an elevator, then up into another big cell outside the courtroom.

My attorney had a guard pull me out of the cell and wheel me down a small hallway into a room where she was sitting. I said to her, "Did drug court decide to take me?"

She said, "No, I'm sorry." Then she said, "The judge is offering you three third-degree felonies for attempted distribution if you'll plead guilty."

I told her, "Well, if drug court won't take me, then of course I'll take the three nickels." I then said, "I would have no chance at beating the three first-degree felonies, why would they offer me three thirds?"

She told me she wasn't sure, but she thought it must have something to do with President Obama's big movement to push programs over prisons, and they always offered things to avoid court. She then said, "I'm going to try to get you out today."

When the guard wheeled me back to the big cell, I started to remember back to my nights spent at Clyde and Jeanne's, studying the book, *A Course in Miracles*, and remembering good old eleventh-step Clyde, telling me that whenever I was going to a place, that was scary; or if there was a difficult task or a test, I should send pink light up to my God and imagine him/her sending it back and filling that difficult room with this pink light. Clyde said, "Make everything in that room pink—everything!"

So that is what I was going to do. As I sat back in my chair in that cell, there were about twenty other guys in there with me still. I was about to send pink light up to the heaven when it dawned on me that I didn't remember what the color pink looked like! I'd been in jail for two months, and there was nothing pink here! I racked my brain, trying to remember anything pink, a sweater or a shirt or some pink panties that I had seen, but nothing was coming to my mind. How the hell was I going to send pink light when I couldn't remember what pink looked like?

A guard walked in from the courtroom after they announced the judge. As he shut the door, separating the holding cells from the courtroom, on the back of the metal door was a pink sheet of paper. On the pink paper in black letters, it read, "Jury Duty."

I was so relieved. I first thanked God and then began to send pink light up to the sky. I found it easy to imagine everything in the courtroom was pink as the guard wheeled me in. The judge first asked me if I pled guilty to the three thirds willingly and of my own accord. I said, "Yes, ma'am, your honor, I do."

She then said, "On Monday, the nineteenth of May 2014, Darren H pleads guilty to three accounts of attempted distribution of a controlled substance. Defendant will be sentenced in forty days." As the judge began to ask if I had anything to say, the guard reached up from behind me and unlocked the lever on my right wheel so he could wheel me back out of the courtroom. As the guard reached for my left wheel lever, my attorney started to speak to the judge. When this happened, I reached down and relocked my right wheel. The guard kind of grunted in frustration.

My attorney said, "From 1989 to 1992, Darren did 12-step work in the state prison and the county jail as a volunteer." Then she said, "Darren's volunteer work was for a couple different fellowships, but he was really working for the courts and trying to help the inmates find recovery. I think we owe it to him to let him out today."

The prosecutor immediately stood up, and he kind of laughed and said, "Darren H was arrested for three first-degree felonies. I think he needs to sit in jail for forty more days until his sentencing!"

As the guard began to reach down to unlock my wheel again, the judge spoke up and said, "Yes, Mr. H, I do feel like we owe it to you to release you today. I'll see you back in forty days for sentencing."

As the court clerk wrote up my pink "get out of jail" voucher, I looked behind me, grinning ear to ear at Teddy, my mom, and Kimberly in the audience, and a couple rows behind them was my stepmom, Patrica, and my dad. I think many family reunions happen in courtrooms.

My ride back to the jail on the bus was, I'm sorry to say, kind of fun. I think in sharing my story and my pink voucher with the other jailbirds, it gave them hope. When I got back to my section, the commissary had come. The guard asked me if I wanted him to send it back since I was leaving in a couple hours. I told him, "No, but thank you, I'd like to munch out." Knowing I could never eat my entire commissary in two hours, I thought it would be nice to share with my new friends who couldn't afford their own snacks. With all my excitement and thoughts of tasting a cigarette, I forgot the jail rules and walked into another guy's cell. I wasn't thinking. I was just talking to him and followed him into his room.

The guard yelled at me and said, "Mr. H, get in your cell! You will now be on lockdown until you leave!"

Being unable to share my commissary meant I would leave it with my celli, but there was no way the guards would let him keep it. Jail rules are so messed up. I loaded all my bedding and notebooks and pens onto my wheelchair and waited for my release. Finally, three hours after I got back from court, I heard the lock release sound on my cell door. I began my walk down the long hallway, pushing my loaded wheelchair like a walker to the booking/release part of the jail. I took off my jumpsuit and my jail issued "tighty-whities" and changed into my boxer shorts and the sweat pants I was arrested in.

I didn't want to call anyone for a ride that might bring dope to celebrate my release, so I called my mother for a ride. I walked over to the gas station to wait for my mom to arrive and I almost didn't buy a pack of cigarettes since it had been sixty days since I'd had one, but then I decided to.

It was so nice being out and it was great to see my mom, but I couldn't get her to stop hugging me. We drove back to her condo, and I was so excited to grab the TV remote when we arrived. The hard plastic felt so good in my hand. I just couldn't stop changing the channels—what a rush! The queen-sized bed upstairs in the guest bedroom felt so big and soft compared to the jail bed I'd been sleeping on for sixty days. The smell of the Colombian coffee as it began to perk downstairs in the kitchen was magical. The little things in life that I always took for granted were making me aware of how blessed I really was.

I called Sara to let her know I was home at my mom's, but there was no answer. I called Teddy, my daughter, and talked for quite a while about what my life was going to entail now. We also talked about Sara's addiction to the heroin and her addiction to the lifestyle. I told Teddy that I felt obligated to help Sara find her way back in to the rooms of recovery but wasn't sure if that was possible. Knowing how I was and knowing that unless I hit a devastating bottom, recovery would never be possible for me; how could it be possible for Sara? Teddy told me that Sara was living in a new place with Kevin and Cory; I kept her in my prayers that night.

The day after my release from jail, I attended the 3:00 p.m. 12-Step meeting at the Alano Club. The meeting was called "The Island of Misfit Toys." I took a sheet of paper to the meeting and wrote the name of the meeting and the date on it. When the Seventh Tradition basket came around, I put the sheet of paper in the basket. After the meeting, I retrieved my signed paper. I did the same thing five times a week for the next forty days. It felt nice being back in the rooms of recovery. I knew so many people from my decade-and-a-half spent here.

After that first meeting, I took a bus down to St. Mary's treatment center and got on the waiting list to get a bed in treatment. St. Mary's location had moved from when I paroled there in 1997. They were in a big Catholic house with a good-sized yard with a pond and a smoke lodge out back. Now they were in a little white bricked office building that used to be where my pediatrician was when I was young.

I started to once again feel the high that comes from bettering myself. My feelings were mixed because I was pretty scared about what would happen when I was sentenced. Part of me wanted to run away and hide, but part of me believed that this was all part of my recovery. I felt so much fear, but I knew that was just my ego. My spirit felt like I could be part of not only my recovery but that I could be here to help others as well.

My daughter and her boyfriend, Dan, and I went fishing up in the Uinta Mountains at Strawberry Reservoir in the middle of June. We had a great day fishing. We caught a lot of big trout, browns, and rainbows. They told me that Teddy, my baby girl, was going to have a baby. Teddy said, "I'm four months pregnant, so in November, you will be a grandpa."

I was so excited for Teddy. She always wanted to have a baby, but there were some complications that made it real hard for her to get pregnant. I asked her if she wanted a baby girl or a baby boy. She said, "It doesn't matter, but if it's a girl, I'm going to name her Marie-Lynn because Dan's middle name is Marie, and mine is Lynn."

I asked her what she would name a son. She told me she didn't know. I got the idea that she wanted a daughter.

On Thursday, July 10, 2014, I got a bed at St. Mary's, and on Monday, the fourteenth, I was sentenced. When I went to sentencing, I brought my acceptance letter to St. Mary's and all the signed papers from all the 12-step meetings that I had attended since my release from jail. One of the RC's (Resident Coordinators) from St. Mary's drove me over to the courthouse that day. My mom and dad both showed up, and so did my daughter and Sara. I gave all my paperwork to my attorney to give to the judge. She made a copy of all of it so the prosecutor could have a copy in front of him as well.

I was so nervous I was shaking inside, but it was nice having my loved ones there. My name was called out, "Darren H."

I grabbed my cane and began my walk up the aisle. When I got to the front of the courtroom, the prosecutor stood up and faced me; he then reached his hand toward me. I quickly jumped back in defense as he smiled at me. I looked down at his open hand, then stretched my arm out and shook his hand. With his other hand, he lifted up all the paperwork that my attorney gave him and said, "This is exactly what we want people to do, exactly."

The judge then sentenced me to complete the treatment center I was in and then put me on thirty-six months' probation.

The following day, I call my new state-issued probation officer. His name was Bryan Peterson, and he was a hard ass. The first thing he said when I called and introduced myself was, "Have you been drinking?"

I explained my problems with my voice and about my head injury. I also told him that I hadn't had a drink since the eighteenth of July 1995. It was like he didn't even hear what I said. His response was, "You have a drug and alcohol clause in your order from the judge. You need to come here and give a UA now!" Then he said, "If you're dirty, I will be taking you to jail!"

I explained to him that I lived in a treatment center and I peed in a cup every other day for them here. I then told him that I would have to have a staff member bring me down because I was still on my first two-week restriction and couldn't leave the facility unaccompanied. He told me that I didn't have to come down but I needed to give him the staff's phone number, and he showed up at St. Mary's the next day.

Life in treatment was nice. They drove the residences to a 12-step meeting every night. The classes that I attended were all about discovering the issues that caused me to drink and use drugs. It was all just a refresher course for me. I had learned all the material before. I really got to thinking, though, on why I ever went back to that life, knowing how I would end up—*jails, institutions, or death*, oh my. I was pretty sure it had to do with the first step or my not completely doing a first step. I guess I must not have been convinced that I was powerless and thought I could do it again without consequence; I was mistaken.

After my two-week restriction had ended at St. Mary's, I walked over to a meeting in a church a couple blocks away. I heard a man share who had twenty years of sobriety. He shared about his life and his ego. His words somehow led me to believe that he had studied the course in miracles. I approached him after the meeting and asked him if he studied the course. He told me a little but that his wife was way in to it and that she used to study with Clyde and Jeanne.

I told him about my relationship with Clyde and Jeanne and how we moved course to my house when Clyde got sick. I had a real good feeling about this guy, so I asked him to be my sponsor. His name was Charles. I then got a friend request on social media from an old friend of my daughter's mom from back in the high school days. Her name was Kim, and I always thought she was fine, but she was my girlfriend's BFF, so it was always a "no fly zone." It was sure nice to hear from her.

Charles was a real good sponsor. He had me call him every day. I explained to Charles about all my years in recovery but was afraid that I keep missing something. We immediately got into the book and the steps. I explained my desire to him to make sure I did a complete and thorough first step. So Charles had me write not only my actions down on paper but also the way I felt inside when I did these actions. Doing this sure made me very aware of my triggers. I was then asked to write out my answers to the following questions: How is your life powerless to drugs and alcohol? In which ways has your life become unmanageable? What other areas of your life do you find yourself powerless? Do you really want your life to be manageable? Tell me what the term "Admission of Hopelessness" means to you?

At the end of every step was a quote from *A Course in Miracles*: "All miracles mean life, and God is the giver of life. His voice will direct you very specifically. You will be told all you need to know."

Charles told me that we would work the steps as fast as I wanted to. After I completed the first step and certainly had the desire to get on the second one, but I was so busy with treatment, it was a few weeks before I could complete it. The questions for step 2 were: Are you God? Defiance is the outstanding characteristic of most junkies and drunks. can you relate? Can you remember times in your life where defiance turned out to be the wrong move? Explain. Do you believe you are insane? Did your actions while using make you feel insane? Do you want to be restored to sanity? "Miracles are expressions of love, but they may not always have observable effects."

I graduated treatment in three and a half months. I left St. Mary's on October 31. Charles and I did my third step just before I left treatment. The questions were: If there were three men in a boat fishing and one man makes a *decision* to jump out of the boat and into the lake, how many men are left in the boat (answer at the end)? What does the term *willingness* mean to you? Have you ever regretted turning your will over to somebody? Has your will given you the control and serenity that you really want? Do you believe that turning your will over to the care of God gives you more control? Explain. Are you able to depend on your parents? Can your friends depend on you (Answer: Three men left in the boat; he changed his mind).

"God loves us no matter what. We are his children and he will always unconditionally love us."

Not having much of an income any longer, just my monthly SSI deposit, made my paying rent anywhere quite hard. Thank God my mother offered me the guestroom in her condo. She was in Oahu most of the time anyway. My driver's license was still suspended from when I got busted selling that Roxy to Gentri back in 2012. I could get it back, but it would cost me $1,000, and I'd have to go take the test again. So I got in the habit of riding the bus and walked a few blocks every day to get to my meetings.

Kim finally came over and saw me. She was still as fine as I'd remembered. We shared a long passionate kiss; it was nice. On the seventh of November, my daughter turned twenty-seven, and on the tenth of November 2014, my granddaughter, Marie-Lynn, was born. She was the prettiest little baby. She weighed five pounds and twelve ounces. As I held her in my arms, I remembered how good I felt when Teddy Bear was born. I was also reminded of the many things in life that got me high the right way.

My sponsor told me that the fourth step was about writing, writing, and then writing some more. He said, "It's about digging deep inside yourself and finding out why you want to be so miserable." The questions I was to write about were: Are you angry? If so, why? Are you sad? If so, why? Do you feel guilty? Why? What have been your best experiences in life? What have been your worst experiences in life? Do you have any hidden secrets that you don't want to share? Do you see how sharing those would be beneficial to you? Do you believe you're a worthwhile person? I think you are, but tell me why you think you are or why you think you aren't? Do you think your drug addiction has caused others to feel differently about you? If so, tell me about how or what that makes you feel?

"Miracles are both beginnings and endings, so they alter the temporal order. They are always affirmations of rebirth, which seem to go back but really go forward. They undo the past in the present, and thus release the future."

The fifth step was about sharing my fourth step with my sponsor and God. The sixth step came at a perfect time; well, they all seemed to. I was starting to build a relationship with Kim and I needed to be reminded about my intentions. The questions on my sixth step were: Has God removed your obsession to use? Has that obsession been replaced with something else? Explain. Do you have faith that God will remove all your defects of character? Do you want all your defects removed? Do you think you could cope with so much change all at once? In my life, I believe that things happen in God's time, not mine. How do you feel or think about that?

"Miracles transcend the body. They are sudden shifts in to invisibility away from the bodily level. That is why they heal."

The sixth made me eager to jump onto the seventh. My questions were: Define the word *humble*. Does your time spent in misery make you humble? Do you feel that your time spent feeling bad will improve the rest of your life? Explain. Do you think you are becoming more tolerant? In which ways are you becoming more tolerant? Do you see how being a rebel and being humble contradict each other? Explain. Is your will to stay clean and sober stronger than your will to use? Explain. Do you believe that humbling yourself could actually help others? Tell me about that. Define the word *shortcoming*. Do you see how the sixth step was about being or getting ready for the changes that were about to happen? Step 7 is an action step. It is the way to show a conscience awareness of defects and humbly asking for help to remove these defects.

"Miracles are healing because they supply a lack; they are performed by those who temporarily have more for those who temporarily have less."

The eighth-step questions were: Do you forgive yourself for all the pain and suffering that you put yourself through and why? In making a list of all the people you have harmed, I've always found it best to put yourself at the top of the list. Once you have forgiven yourself, the rest comes pretty easy. Define the word *harm*. In the making of a list, you must include people that you've harmed emotionally, physically, and spiritually. Do you think it's possible to know all the people you've harmed in your life? Be prepared because as you start to do your ninth step, you will remember more names to add to your eighth-step list. People that are unreachable need to go on your list; this is for you. We will deal with the unmailable letters in the next step.

"A miracle is a universal blessing from God through me to all my brothers. It is the privilege of the forgiven to forgive."

There weren't a lot of questions for the ninth step, just words of motivation: Remember that making amends to anyone is not worth risking your sobriety, because without your sobriety, you have nothing. I hope that through the time you've been sober, you've learned to deal with change, for that's what this step is about. Not only will the way you feel about yourself change, but also the way that others, not only the ones you make amends to, but all others feel about you. The only way to be free of your past, present, and life you have in front of you is to give it to God. The only real question on this step is, are you ready? Sometimes making amends can be as easy as saying, "I'm sorry." Other times, it can be a bit harder. Setting up payment plans was what my ninth step mostly entailed, but with most the people I owed money to, once that they saw that my intention was right, they didn't really care about the money. My credit card bills and delinquencies at the banks were a different story. They wanted their money. Remember, the satisfaction needs take place in your heart. Making amends to people that are no longer alive is as difficult as you want it to be. Once you find the ability to forgive yourself, it becomes easier to see how they could also forgive you.

"The miracle dissolves error because the Holy Spirit identifies error as false or unreal. It is the same as saying that by perceiving light darkness automatically disappears."

The tenth step questions were: Tell me what you've learned about, "emotional balance" after working the first nine steps? Tell me about the changes that you've seen in yourself? Do you see things in your life that you still need to work on? Still need to change? Tell me about that. Do you find yourself tired from dealing with emotional stress? At night before you go to sleep, you need to go through your memories of the day of all of your actions, remembering the wrongs and rights that happened. Do you see the harm in getting angry? Even if justified? When there is a problem, pray about it then let it go.

"The miracle makes no distinction among degrees of misperception. It is a device for perception correction, effective quite apart from either the degree or the direction of the error. This is its true indiscriminateness."

The eleventh step questions were: Do you have a conscience contact with your higher power? If not, do you want one? Prayer and meditation are good for all people because it puts the heart and the head on the same page. Do you believe that? Is it easier for you to feel peaceful when it's quiet? How about dark? Meditation is about getting or being where you are most at peace. It's about shutting everything off and just listening. I believe prayer is about talking to God, and meditation is about listening. If you have a method that works for you, then that's great. If not here, a suggestion or what I do.

In the morning after I wake up, but before I leave my bed, I close my eyes and ask God to share his will with me throughout my day and ask him to keep me clean and sober. At night, when I get back to bed, I run through the happenings of my day and then pray and thank him for my miracles and for keeping me clean and sober. Then I light a candle and turn out the light. I begin to clear my head, only seeing darkness, except that shimmering light from the candle and then begin to count my breaths.

In the beginning, I was unable to clear my head, so I would imagine the repetitive action of sheep jumping over a fence, one after another, and I'd see a man with long hair counting the jumping sheep. I would breathe in every time a sheep would jump and out when it landed. My meditation always followed my prayers. My meditation started at two minutes a night for the first week, then five minutes a night the second week, then moved up to ten minutes my third week, and has since remained at the length. There is no wrong or right way to pray and meditate. I have found for me that if I get into a routine and do it twice a day, every day, things don't seem to bother me as much, and it has become easier to let things go.

"Miracles are examples of right thinking, aligning your perceptions with truth as God created it."

The joy that came to me from getting through the paperwork on the twelfth step is actually indescribable. I guess I would say the first eleven steps were the work or the waiting game. Step 12 was the reward or the high. It's kind of hard to call the first eleven steps work because they were all so rewarding. The questions for step 12 were: Have you felt the joy that has come from helping another? What does the term "spiritual awakening" mean to you? 12-step work can be as easy as being in regular attendance at your meetings. But when you're called to go out to help someone who is drunk or on drugs, it's very important that you don't go alone. Do you understand why? Each night when I pray, I ask to be relieved of pride that might sound kind of funny, but I do that because of my ego. Tell me what you think I mean by that? Do you see how each one of the 12 steps are a way to chip away at your ego and that each one is a process for setting up a format to live a clean and sober and happy life? This might take a while, but go through all your written steps, starting with 1 and ending with 11, letting me know what working each step has shown you about living life. The biggest thing that I've received from working the 12 steps is the ability to accept life on life's terms.

Nothing, absolutely nothing, happens in God's world by mistake. I need to understand that things happen that I don't agree with or understand, and that's life. How do you feel about that? After you get done with the twelfth step, it would be most beneficial to you to find someone to sponsor and work the steps with them as I worked them with you. Don't worry if you can't find someone to sponsor.

Just keep attending your meeting and reaching your hand out; it will happen. "God grant us the serenity to accept the things we cannot change, the courage to change the things we can, and the wisdom to know the difference."

"The miracle compares what you have made with creation, accepting what is in accord with it as true, and rejecting what is out of accord as false."

Just after finishing my step-work, I celebrated my one year being clean and sober. I spoke and received chips at a few meetings. My mother was returning from Oahu soon, and I told her that I would be moved out of her condo by the time she got home. Having such a little bit of money every month was hard, but my SSI checks were only about $700 a month. So I sent a message out on social media. It read, "Single guy looking for a sober place to rent in the Salt Lake area. Need it soon, any ideas?"

The very next day, I got a personal message that said, "Darren, my name is Beatriz, and I heard you speak in a meeting the other night. I have a room for rent for $400 per month." She then left her phone number.

I called her immediately and actually moved in two days later. Beatriz was a great roommate, and the guy that she was seeing, Charles, was a great program friend of mine. The meetings I usually attend are so big that perhaps I had seen her before but just didn't remember. I kind of doubt I had seen her before. She was stunning, and I don't usually forget stunners.

We lived in a nice little apartment in Sugarhouse, just around the corner from Fellowship Hall where there were lots of meetings. Walking to my meetings was good because I still didn't have my driver's license back. Kim, who I was seeing a lot of these days, offered to lend me the $1,000 I needed to get my license back, but it felt kind of weird borrowing money like that. My probation officer and his partner stopped by every couple of weeks and did a quick search of my room—such an embarrassment.

At the end of the summer in 2015, I did borrow the money from Kim and got my driver's license back and my old Subaru that I got busted in a few years back was sitting in the back-storage lot at my mom's condo. It needed a lot of work. Eric, a guy I met in jail and who I was sponsoring, had an old beater car that he was letting me drive. I was so broke all the time. After rent, cigarettes, and the few bills I paid each month, I had no money for gas. So the car just basically sat there.

My probation officer didn't really like the idea of me driving. So that, of course, made me want to drive even more.

My mom called me in the fall from Oahu and said, "I have enough miles saved with Delta that I can get you a ticket over here for a couple weeks." My little sister, Josie, and her husband, Terry, and my three nephews lived in a condo on the south end of Oahu in Hawaii Kia. I was so excited that I told everyone that I was going. Mom told me to ask my probation officer when it would be best to go.

I called Bryan Peterson, my PO, to ask him when would be the best time to go, assuming he would say, "After your appointment on the first of the month." But no, Bryan my probation officer said, "You can't go, you can't leave the state at all while you're on probation!"

I called my mother and told her the bad news. She was upset, and I was too, but what do you do?

A few weeks later, my friend, Dan, called me and told me that his work was hiring. Dan, a guy I've known since high school that has been in and out of the program so often, I actually sponsored him back in 2008 and sold him heroin a few years after that. Dan kept me informed about Sara, Kevin, and Corey, for that is where he bought his black these days. Dan worked for Precision Assembly down in Orem, Utah. I told Dan that I had no skills at anything and asked him, "Why would they hire a convicted felon?"

He told me that they didn't care. They just need people to run tests on these circuit boards. So I e-mailed them my resume, and they immediately called me back for an interview. I was hired on the first part of November, and I drove Eric's car to work every day at 3:00 p.m. and then off at 11:30 p.m. It was about a twenty-five-mile drive to Orem.

After I got my first paycheck, Eric and I got my old Subaru working. I actually had a driver's license, a registration, and insurance all at the same time. People in my old world refer to that as a trifecta, and they probably thought I'd be running for president next.

My probation officer was very pleased. I think he even smiled when I told him at my appointment in the first week of December. He told me, "You're doing so well with your probation that I'd like to terminate you." He then said, "It's up to Judge Mills, though I will schedule you to stand before her in a couple of weeks."

That was certainly the best appointment I ever had with him.

Two weeks later, I stood in front of Judge Ruby Mills, and she said as she looked down at the paperwork, "This is great, Darren, you're doing so well." Then she looked over at the prosecution side of the room and said, "Does the state have anything to say?"

The prosecutor stood up and said, "We think Darren should now be on county probation."

I felt the hair on the back of my neck stand up; who the hell did he think he was? Oh, well, county probation was a walk in the park compared to state probation, so I thought, *It's progress, not perfection.*

Then the Honorable Judge Ruby Mills spoke again, and she said, "No, I think Darren is doing great with his life. I'm just going to terminate his probation." Then she said, "Darren, have you anything to say?"

I was grinning ear to ear and said, "Thank you, Your Honor, and Merry Christmas."

She then gave me the prettiest smile as I turned and walked out of the courtroom. It was truly a miracle. I got busted for three first-degree felonies, each holding a term of five years to life in prison, and now seventeen months later, I'm totally off paper, totally off. Who says there's not a God?

Soon as I got home from court, I called my family in Oahu and told them the great news. Then I said, "As soon as I've been at my job for ninety days, I get five days of paid vacation. So I will work five days, then have two off, then use my five days' vacation, then have two days off so I can be gone for nine days." My mom flew back to Salt Lake for Christmas and was going to fly back to Oahu with me.

The middle of February 2016, we flew from Salt Lake International Airport to the Los Angeles International Airport, which by the way has no smoking room, and then flew to Honolulu on the island of Oahu. My brother-in-law, Terry, picked us up at the airport; he put a lei around my neck and gave me a big hug. My sister, Josie, and my three nephews—Hayden, Nate, and Dreyson—were all up and waiting for us when we arrived. I was dressed in a sweater and jeans. It was like twenty degrees when we left Salt Lake, and now the temperature was eighty degrees and it was after midnight.

In the morning, after we had breakfast, I asked my sister for a ride to the store. I bought seven postcards to send to Teddy, Kim, my dad, my three sisters in Utah, and the last one to send to Bryan Peterson at AP&P, my last probation officer. We did so many things in the next nine days and saw so many beautiful rock formations and so many green mountains and so many beautiful beaches. We even drove up to the north shore one day to watch the surfers on those big waves and saw an outside concert in downtown Honolulu. The band, Green, was performing. I was able to look AA up in the phone book for a schedule and was able to attend a couple meetings while I was there.

I was in paradise, but I sure did miss my Kim and couldn't wait to get back and see her. I flew back by myself. Mom was staying, and who could blame her? It was so nice in Oahu and still so cold in Salt Lake when I got back.

Work at Precision Assembly was not really hard, just a lot of repetition. The drive to and from Orem every day was kind of hard on the old Subaru. Kim and I had decided to move in together. We got a place in Sandy, Utah, which cut my drive time in half to Orem. I had to go ten miles in the other direction to get to my meetings every day, but that was fine. I ran in to an old program friend named Kevin one day at a meeting, and he asked me to sponsor him. I asked him to call me every day for a week, and I told him, "If you do that, then I'll get you going on the first step."

Kevin did call me every day. He actually still does, so I started him on his first step. I worked the steps with my sponsee the same way my sponsor worked them with me. It's so rewarding to be able to work with someone and to freely pass on what I was so freely given.

Dan showed up to work one night in early October and told me that Sara had passed away. He said that she was back in her room at Kevin and Cory's house and she did a shot of heroin that was just too big. He then told me that they didn't find her for at least a day. Nobody wanted to bother her. They thought she was just sleeping. When they did go in her room, she was on the floor and her head had been bleeding. Apparently, she overdosed on the bed and then fell off and hit her head. I felt so bad for the role I played in Sara's life. Dan then told me that, "Heroin overdose is a very peaceful way to die. By the time your lungs fill with fluid and you drown, you're fast asleep."

I said, "That's wonderful, Dan, maybe Sara's daughter can stitch that on a pillow for Sara's mom!"

Kim and I had to move out of the apartment in Sandy because they were tearing down the complex to build something else. We moved into a house in Rose Park, which is on the north side of Salt Lake. My drive to Orem was now ten miles further than when I lived with Beatrice in Sugarhouse. The house we moved to was owned by Kim's sister's husband's mom.

Being a convicted felon with awful credit made my choices on where I live very limited. Kim also had no credit, so having family with a house for rent was a blessing. It was kind of an expensive blessing because rent was $300 more than it was at our last place because we were in a house now with a lawn that I had to mow and sidewalks I had to shovel snow off of. Kim had a hard time finding work, so my money was gone so fast. We started fighting a bit more than couples usually do, but we would always make up, and that was always fun. One day, I decided to move out and go stay back at my mom's condo. Kim went and stayed with her boys, Stephen and Bret.

I really started hating my job and that long drive to and from work every day. So I started looking for work here in the valley. I found the same problems that I have always had in finding employment—I talk funny, walk funny, not fast enough on a keyboard, then there were all the felonies. The number was now at six third-degree felonies. My sister, Kimberly, called me and told me of a treatment center that was hiring over by the Alano Club where I hit my meetings and that I should drop off my resume over there sometime.

I did drop a copy of my resume at this treatment center but was unable to talk to anyone. I went to open the door, and it was locked, so I rang the bell, and a girl came to the door and opened it and said, "May I help you?"

I said, "Yeah, could you please give this to whoever it goes to? And can I use your bathroom?"

She took the resume from my hand and said, "I'll have to take you up to the second floor for a bathroom, so hold on a minute."

I told her, "Never mind, I'm fine."

A couple weeks went by, and no call back's or luck finding work. So I went to a staffing agency run by the Mormon Church. I met a very nice man named Perry who scheduled me a time to come back and take some kind of skills test.

Just before I left my mom's condo for my skill's test appointment, I got a call from a lady named Alison. She did human resources at this treatment center by the club where I'd dropped off my resume. Alison wanted me to come in for an interview the next day. I wrote down her name and phone number and put it in my pocket. I then left for my appointment. When I got there, I told Perry, my staffing counselor, about my scheduled interview tomorrow, and he said, "Do you want me to call her? We could even pay your salary for the first two weeks until you get comfortable with the job." He then asked me how much it paid. I told him, and he said, "Well, we will pay you three dollars less than that, but you'll get your foot in the door."

I said, "Okay, yes, please call her."

It felt very uncomfortable sitting there, listening to Perry tell Alison my defects. When the call ended, he told me I still an interview with Alison tomorrow and they were hiring an RC. I said, "What the hell? Oh, excuse me, Perry, what the heck is an RC?"

He told me he had no idea, so we called around and looked on the Internet for the definition of RC, but we never could find it. I just planned on faking it or asking someone in the treatment center before I met Alison.

I wore suit pants and a dress shirt with a tie and dress shoes that hurt my feet. I was twenty minutes early and was so nervous. I chain-smoked a few cigarettes before I went to the door. The door was answered by a young guy that was nicely dressed, not as nice as me but nicely casual. He led me in and over to a couch at the bottom of the stairs and told me to wait.

A few minutes later, Alison came down the stairs and said, "Would you rather take the elevator up?"

I nodded my head yes, then followed her into the elevator. We rode up to the second floor, and I followed her to her office. Alison offered me a beverage, but I said, "No, I'm fine." Then the interview started. She lifted up my resume and told me that she was very impressed with my degree in interdisciplinary studies, emphasis in sociology and psychology. She then said, "Not many RCs have degrees."

I said, "What is an RC?"

Alison smiled at me and said, "Resident Coordinator."

I told her, "Oh, I thought so," but I don't think she was fooled.

The interview went well. I seemed to answer all the questions right. She then asked me if I hung out at the Alano Club. I told her, "Yes, on and off for about thirty years now."

She then said, "Do you know Dan?" She motioned with her hand for Dan to come into her office. I did know Dan, not real well, but what's important was Dan knew me. I always had a real strong drunk-a-log or junk-a-log; a lot of people got a real strong message when I would share.

I stood up and shook Dan hands as he said, "Hey, Darren, it's good to see you."

As the interview ended, Alison said those dreaded words, "Now it's time for your background check."

As I felt the hope inside me start to leave, I turned my head to the side and mumbled the word, "Fuck!" Then I turned back and faced Alison and said, "I have six third-degree felonies, four for attempted distribution and two for possession."

Alison said, "Only drug charges?"

I said, "Well, yeah, that's right."

Alison then said to me as she stood up and reached her hand out to shake mine, "Welcome aboard!"

I could not stop smiling as I was introduced to my RC manager, Lyla, and taken downstairs and introduced to the day shift RCs and shown where the residents lived. I was then told to return tomorrow morning to get my picture taken for my badge and get my schedule.

The next day when I returned, I did all the paperwork involved with getting a real job where you pay taxes and have to dress and act a certain way. I was a middle-aged man who finally felt like a grown up, and it felt well. Over the next week, I met the weekend RC manager, Clyde, and Bret, the clinical director, and the different therapists in occupational therapy and recreational therapy. I also met different substance-abuse counselors, psychiatrists, medical doctors, and nurses and six or eight different Resident Coordinators.

After working for a few months, I was asked to attend a training class upstairs. The class was on building a bridge between the mind and the body, which I must say I had never heard of before. This was the therapy that they used most at the treatment center, so I was very eager to learn. The professor that came and taught the class talked about the different parts of the brain and how most people in their drug use are using the primitive part of the brain for decision-making. I was taught that using the executive part of the brain would not only help one make better decisions but also feel better about themselves.

I then learned how to switch from the primitive part of the brain to the executive part. It was about closing my eyes and breathing deeply and inviting my source or my God in. I was told I could even imagine a peaceful time or place. This was exactly what I had learned twenty years ago from Clyde and Jeanie in the course in miracles. The primitive part of the brain was the energy of the *ego*, and the Executive part was the energy of the *spirit*. It was all about the decision on which energy you wanted to control you, watching all the magic happen and the patients change so much just by taking the time to breathe and change the flow of energy or the part of the brain that they're using.

My days are all pretty similar. I get to work and make sure all the patients are up and having breakfast. Goals group happens next where each of them talks about what they'd like to accomplish today.

I then drive them to the gym to work out for an hour. Then we get back from the gym, and throughout the rest of the day is when the magic happens, for me anyway! Before and after all the groups that happen, I get one on one time with these addicts and alcoholics. I'm able to hear about their lives, the ups and downs that they have experienced. I share with them about me and about my life and my recovery. Working here is truly a miracle for me, and I am so proud to be part of this team. All of the people I've met and began to love and admire at the treatment center where I work are givers of hope.

Today is the nineteenth of March 2019, my five-year clean and sober anniversary. I hand written most of this book while I was in jail five years ago, and it has taken me forever to type it out. I just lack the coordination to type with more than my one finger. I have been working in treatment for a little over twenty months now, and it brings me such a joy to carry the message. My hope in writing my story is that somebody can learn from my experiences and save themselves from having to waste their time and their valuable brain cells…

About the Author

*D*arren *H.* was born in Salt Lake City, Utah in July of 1969. A graduate of Utah State University, with a major in Interdisciplinary Studies, emphasis in Sociology and Psychology. Currently a Resident Coordinator in a Residential Treatment Center for Addicts and Alcoholics.

www.ingramcontent.com/pod-product-compliance
Lightning Source LLC
Chambersburg PA
CBHW020855110425
24871CB00002B/129